BOAT
Owner's Manual

Published by

TECHNICAL PUBLICATIONS

INTERTEC PUBLISHING CORPORATION
P.O. Box 12901, Overland Park, Kansas 66212

The publisher has exercised reasonable care in compiling the information contained in this manual. The Publisher does not guarantee the applications set forth in this manual to the extent that the operation of a boat and its accessories may be subject to outside influences or factors which cannot be reasonably foreseen. The publisher shall in no way be liable for damages of any description to persons or property, whether incidental or consequential or otherwise related to the use of this manual and in no event shall the liability of the publisher exceed the price paid for this manual.

CONTENTS

PREFACE

This **Boat Owner's Manual** is an introduction to the world of boating...and more specifically, *your boat.* We've included a variety of information on boating topics (especially boating necessities) for veteran as well as first-time boaters, so you can better understand your boat...and the boats around you.

Most of the information in this manual will be of use to all pleasureboat owners, though this book has been specifically written for the owners of outboard, inboard, stern drive and jet drive pleasureboats under 26 feet in length (in keeping with current Coast Guard practice, all pleasureboats powered by gasoline engines will be referred to as "motorboats" throughout this manual).

A primary goal of this publication is to impress upon the boat owner the importance of thinking and practicing **safety** when boating. Much of the information you'll find here is concerned with **safe boat operation,** but we can convey this information to you only if you read this manual thoroughly. *The boat operator is ultimately responsible for the safety of his passengers...his boat...and himself.* Included in this manual are color-coded safety boxes to warn you of conditions or procedures that may not be safe. Heed these warnings and act accordingly.

We hope you'll find this manual an important reference tool as you and your boat become acquainted (and that the book remains a reference source long after your get-acquainted period).

We wish you many enjoyable and safe hours of boating.

The Editors
Technical Publications

YOUR DEALER

Selecting a dealership can be just as important as selecting the right motorboat. If you intend to buy your boat from a dealer, evaluate the dealership as well as the boats. If you don't buy the boat from a dealer, first check out the dealers who service and stock parts for your rig. In some localities, it might require some extra mileage to find the good dealer who will work with you, but it will be worth it if you must depend heavily on a dealer.

When evaluating a dealership, consider the following points:

1. Is the dealership clean and well-organized?
2. Are the personnel courteous and are the salespeople, service department people and parts department people knowledgeable?
3. Are the service and parts department areas clean, well-organized and efficient?
4. Are the service and parts department hours convenient for you?
5. Ask the dealership for recent customer references and ask the Better Business Bureau for comments.

Try to build a good business relationship with the dealership personnel. Note the word BUSINESS here. They are there to make a living just like everyone else. Don't monopolize their time with unnecessary chitchat when there are other customers waiting. When you enter the dealership for parts or service, know as much about the part you need or the problem you are having as you possibly can. Insufficient information can make the job more difficult for the partsman or mechanic and may force you to travel home for the needed information.

Be just as friendly to the dealership personnel as you expect them to be to you. This friendly attitude may result in some special help in the future.

BOAT IDENTIFICATION

CLASSES

Motorboats are classified by overall boat length. The overall length is measured from the foremost part of the boat to the aftermost part of the boat, parallel to the centerline and not including the attachments. An outboard motor is NOT included in the measurement.

Classifications are: less than 16 feet, 16 feet but less than 26 feet, 26 feet but less than 40 feet and 40 feet to 65 feet.

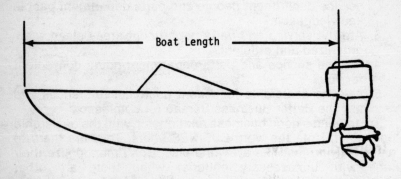

Boat Length

DRIVE TYPES

Outboard Motor Boat

The outboard motor is a complete assembly with the powerhead mounted on top of the lower-drive unit. The motor is mounted on the transom on the outside of the boat hull.

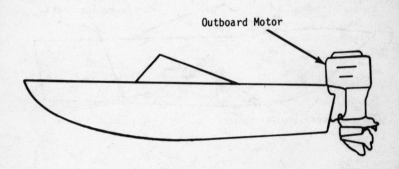

Outboard Motor

Inboard/Outdrive Boat

The inboard/outdrive boat is commonly referred to as a stern-drive boat. The marine engine is mounted on the inside of the boat hull. The drive unit is mounted to the rear of the engine and is located on the outside of the boat hull.

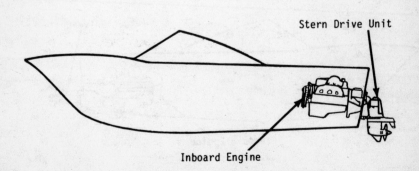

Stern Drive Unit

Inboard Engine

Inboard Boat

The marine engine and drive unit are mounted on the inside of the boat hull. A propeller shaft extends from the rear of the drive unit to the outside of the boat hull where the propeller is mounted.

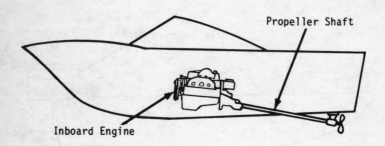

Propeller Shaft

Inboard Engine

Jet Drive Boat

Driven by a marine engine, the impeller of the jet drive unit draws water in through an intake grill at the bottom of the boat hull. The impeller then forces the water out through a stern thrust nozzle at a high rate of speed creating a propulsive thrust to propel the boat.

A set of controls and a thrust gate are used to control braking, maneuvering and direction.

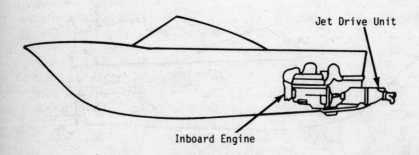

Jet Drive Unit

Inboard Engine

HULL TYPES

The potential speed of a boat depends as much on the design of the boat's hull as upon the power of the motor. When selecting a hull type certain considerations should be made:

1. Are you willing to sacrifice a soft ride for maximum performance?
2. Are you willing to sacrifice some performance for a softer ride?
3. What type of water will you be operating in?

You must choose a hull type that will best serve your boating needs. Although there are many individual hull types, most boat hulls will fall into one of two broad categories: the displacement hull and the planing hull.

When not moving, any type of hull will displace its own weight in the water. But, because of the heavily rounded side chines of the displacement hull, most of the water support is permitted to leak out from under the hull. The escaping water will keep the displacement hull at nearly its standing depth when under way. As a result, the hull will have a plowing effect through the water which will increase the hull drag and lower the top speed. The displacement hull maximum speed is limited by the distance between the bow and the stern waves.

The displacement hull is the only logical design for slow moving boats which cannot attain planing speed. It is also more stable in rough water and rides somewhat softer than a planing hull.

At rest the planing hull will displace its own weight in the water. As speed increases, the hull will rise in the water until an adequate speed is reached to put the hull on plane. The planing speed is determined by the amount of hull bottom surface that is still being dragged across the water. There are many factors that will control if and how quickly planing speed is reached, e.g., motor horsepower, propeller shaft trim angle, propeller design and the onboard load and its distribution. To reach maximum speed, the planing hull bottom should be as flat as possible in a lengthwise direction for approximately the last five feet with the transom chine cut clean (sharp edge).

The planing hull will provide maximum performance at planing speed in smooth water, but is very dangerous in rough water and will not, in most cases, provide as soft of a ride as a displacement hull.

The "V" bottom hull combines characteristics of both the displacement hull and the planing hull. A softer ride is obtained with only a small sacrifice of maximum speed. Hull features such as the angle of the "V", keel line radius and the use of a pad or strakes are performance characteristics the hull manufacturer uses to gain a desired effect.

Other hull designs are available on the market with each of them having their own performance characteristics. Be sure you understand how the different hull designs will react when placed under certain water conditions and performance levels. Choose the hull design that will best fit your needs. Following are some hull design variations.

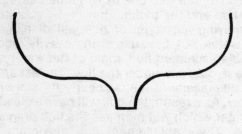

DISPLACEMENT BOTTOM

FLAT BOTTOM WITH HARD CHINE

FLAT BOTTOM WITH SOFT CHINE

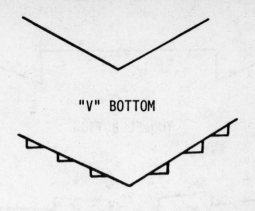

"V" BOTTOM

"V" BOTTOM WITH STRAKES

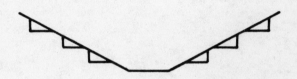

"V" BOTTOM WITH PADS AND STRAKES

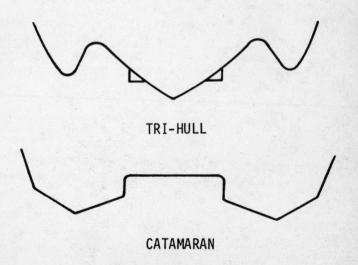

TRI-HULL

CATAMARAN

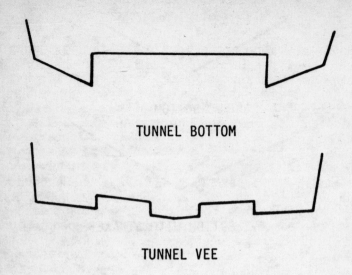

TUNNEL BOTTOM

TUNNEL VEE

CERTIFICATION

Boat certification was started in 1968 by the Boating Industry Association (BIA). BIA set up a certification program for boat manufacturers covering horsepower and load capacity, flotation, steering and fuel systems, compartment ventilation, navigation lights and backfire control. Presently, the National Marine Manufacturers Association (NMMA) administers BIA certification and provides a certification handbook outlining the boat manufacturing certification standards and safety regulations. The boat standards used in the certification handbook are based on the "Standards for Small Craft" published by the American Boat and Yacht Council (ABYC).

Inspections are performed by inspectors from a nationally recognized independent inspection agency. Inspectors check for the NMMA capacity and flotation ratings, and physically inspect each boat model for compliance with the NMMA Certification Handbook. Any defective area found must be reconstructed to comply with certification standards. Only then can a manufacturer attach a NMMA Certification Plate to

---

U.S. COAST GUARD

MAXIMUM CAPACITIES

13 PERSONS OR 1950 LBS

2430 LBS PERSONS, MOTORS, GEAR

125 H.P. MOTOR

THIS BOAT COMPLIES WITH U.S. COAST GUARD SAFETY STANDARDS IN EFFECT ON THE DATE OF CERTIFICATION

MANUFACTURER: HVCHOX BOAT CO.
MODEL: ☐☐☐ COLUMBIA, MICHIGAN

DESIGN COMPLIANCE WITH BIA REQUIREMENTS BELOW IS VERIFIED. MFGR. RESPONSIBLE FOR PRODUCTION CONTROL

LOAD AND H.P. CAPACITY • LEVEL FLOTATION
NAVIGATION LIGHTS • STEERING SYSTEM
COMPARTMENT VENTILATION

NATIONAL MARINE MANUFACTURERS ASSN.

Drawing courtesy of National Marine Manufacturers Assn.

a boat. During the year, without giving any prior warning, inspectors revisit the boat manufacturer's plant to ensure the manufacturer is complying with the certification requirements.

As of November 1, 1972, boats which are in compliance with United States Coast Guard standards must display a plate stating so. Boats that comply with Coast Guard and NMMA or BIA standards will have a single plate that states the boat complies with both sets of standards.

Load capacity varies according to boat type. If your boat does not have a plate stating load capacity, refer to page 27.

Listed in the back of this manual are boat, outboard motor, inboard engine and drive manufacturers. After purchasing a rig or a specific product, new or used, you should contact the manufacturer to inform them of your purchase. You should supply the manufacturer with the necessary personal and product information. This will enable the manufacturer to notify you of any modifications, alterations or other information pertaining to your equipment.

SAFETY

With the popularity of recreational boating continually growing, the waters in which pleasure boats operate are becoming crowded in many areas. This congestion of boats makes the ignorant and careless operator more dangerous.

The operator of a boat is responsible for the safety of the boat and the people onboard. Neglecting this responsibility could jeopardize the safety of your boat, the people onboard or innocent bystanders.

To operate a boat safely, a good operator will:

1. Know how to properly handle his or her boat.
2. Abide by the laws and regulations governing his or her boat and the operational waters.
3. Learn how to correctly use the equipment onboard.
4. Be prepared in case of an emergency.
5. Practice early and careful preparations before starting an outing.
6. At all times, exercise good common sense with safety in mind.
7. Be courteous toward the other boater.

Learning to be a good operator will not interfere with the fun of boating. Being knowledgeable of good boating practices will help make each boat outing safe and enjoyable.

Don't operate a boat while under the influence of alcohol or drugs. Your unclear thinking or slow response could bring about a hazardous situation or keep you from avoiding one.

NOTE

It is a federal offense to operate a boat while under the influence of alcohol or drugs.

Lightheadedness may result after an extended period in the sun. The adverse effect will cause your body to react much in the same manner as being under the influence of alcohol or drugs. Be careful if you are going to operate a boat. Your unclear thinking or slow response could bring about a hazardous situation or keep you from avoiding one.

Use only U.S. Coast Guard approved parts or parts that have been certified for marine use. DO NOT substitute automotive type parts. Automotive type parts do not meet marine safety standards. Using uncertified parts may result in premature failure or a safety hazard.

PERSONAL FLOTATION DEVICES (PFD)

By law there must be at least one Personal Flotation Device (PFD) onboard the boat for every person onboard. The PFDs must be in good condition and the correct size for the intended wearer. All wearable PFDs must be stowed on the boat so they are easily reached while all throwable devices must be immediately available.

All PFDs must be approved by the U.S. Coast Guard. The Coast Guard classifies PFDs according to the following types:

TYPE I PFD. The Type I PFD is an approved wearable device providing the wearer with the greatest amount of protection. This PFD is designed to turn most unconscious people, in the water, from a face down position to a vertical or slightly backward position. The Type I PFD must be able to provide a minimum buoyancy of 22 pounds for an adult and 11 pounds for a child. Type I is recommended for open water boating where there is a possibility of a waiting period before rescue.

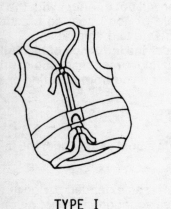

TYPE I

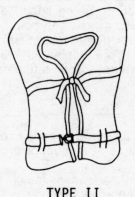

TYPE II

TYPE II PFD. The Type II PFD is an approved wearable device. This PFD is designed to turn an unconscious person, in the water, to a vertical or slightly backward position. The turning action is slower than the Type I PFD and in some cases the Type II may not turn over the wearer. The Type II PFD must be able to provide a minimum buoyancy of 15½ pounds for an adult, 11 pounds for a medium size child and 7 pounds for an infant or small child. Type II is recommended for close off-shore boating where there is usually only a short waiting period before rescue.

TYPE III PFD. The Type III PFD is an approved wearable device. This PFD is designed so a conscious person can position himself or herself in a vertical or slightly backward position. The Type III PFD will have little or no turning ability, but must be able to provide the same minimum buoyancy as the Type II PFD. The Type III PFD will usually allow greater mobility and wearing comfort, which makes it very useful when participating in water skiing, sailing, hunting, fishing or any other water sport. Type III is recommended for lakes, confined waters or close offshore operation.

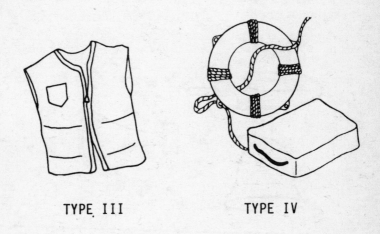

TYPE III   TYPE IV

TYPE IV PFD. The Type IV PFD is any approved device designed to be thrown and held (NOT WORN) by a person in the water. The Type IV PFD must be able to provide a minimum buoyancy of 16½ pounds. Buoyant cushions and ring life buoys are the most common Type IV PFDs.

TYPE V PFD. The Type V PFD is any approved PFD designed for a particular use.

SOUND SIGNALING DEVICES

Sound signaling devices are very important when maneuvering near a hazardous situation, or when encountering low visibility, fog, mist, heavy rain or any other unfavorable weather condition.

There are three basic signaling devices with different styles of each available: the bell, the horn and the whistle. The horn or whistle can be hand, mouth or power operated.

Although no sound signaling device is required on boats less than 39'4" (12 meters), you must still be able to produce an efficient sound signal when foul weather or a hazardous maneuvering situation is encountered. The carrying of a bell, horn or whistle is a good practice as they are recognized signaling devices.

Refer to the *LEGAL REQUIREMENTS* section for the sound signaling device requirements on boats up to but less than 65'6" (20 meters) in length.

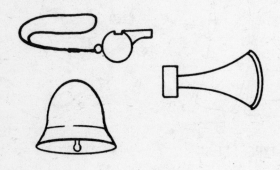

SOUND SIGNALING DEVICES

FIRE EXTINGUISHERS

Every boat powered by a gasoline engine should have a fire extinguisher onboard, although it may not be legally required. The fire extinguisher must be mounted in an easily accessible location and all people onboard should know its location.

Refer to page 31 for the number and size of fire extinguishers which must be carried on motorboats which meet one or more of the following conditions:

1. Inboard engine.
2. Portable fuel tanks stored in closed compartments under thwarts or seats.
3. Double bottom not sealed to hull or not completely filled with flotation materials.
4. Closed living spaces.
5. Combustible or flammable material stored in closed compartments.
6. Permanently installed fuel tanks.

The fire extinguisher label should state that the extinguisher is approved for marine use. Any fire extinguisher produced after January 1, 1965, that is approved for marine use

DRY CHEMICAL FIRE EXTINGUISHER

ISSUE NO.

CLASSIFICATION 2A; 40 B:C
MARINE TYPE USCG TYPE A-SIZE II
TYPE B:C-SIZE I
APPROVAL NO. XXXXXXXXXX

SIMON WENTWORTH & ASSOCIATES
ROCKY ACRES, VIRGINIA 16790

GROSS WGT. 8½ LBS.   MADE IN U.S.A.

will be marked accordingly on the label. Also, if the label is marked U.L. listed, the extinguisher is approved for marine use.

Fire extinguishers are classified according to the type of fire they will extinguish. The types of fires are denoted by a letter classification which appears on the fire extinguisher label. The most common letter classifications and fire types are:

A. Ordinary combustible materials
B. Gasoline, oil or grease
C. Electrical

Any marine fire extinguisher must be classified to extinguish type B fires, although it may also be classified for other type fires as well.

The U.S. Coast Guard classifies fire extinguishers approved for marine use according to the size of the extinguisher. Sizes are designated as roman numerals and sizes I and II are the hand-portable sizes which must be filled to the following capacities:

Classification (Type-Size)	Foam (Gallons)	Carbon Dioxide (Pounds)	Dry Chemical (Pounds)	Halon (Pounds)
B-I	1¼	4	2	2½
B-II	2½	15	10	. . .

LIGHTING

Federal law requires that all boats must display certain lights for night operation. After viewing the arrangement and appearance of your boat lights, an approaching boater should be able to conclude whether he is in a meeting, crossing or overtaking situation and the approximate size of your boat.

There are only three colors of lights used: red, green and white. Red is displayed on the port bow (left side). Green is displayed on the starboard bow (right side). White is usually displayed on the stern (back) of the boat, but may be located at other areas on the boat.

An anchor light is a white light visible for two miles to a boat approaching from any direction. The anchor light must be displayed in a location that is clearly visible.

Lights are measured in points. Each point is 11¼ degrees of a complete circle. There are 32 points in a complete circle of light. For example, a ten-point light can be produced by shading out the remaining 22 points. Shading is used to limit the viewing angle.

Light requirements are dependent upon the boat size and type. Boat manufacturers who supply lights are required to comply with federal requirements. Most manufacturers will comply with both the "Inland" and the "International" requirements. Smaller boats that are not intended for operation in international waters may only meet the Inland requirements.

A boat that complies with the International requirements also meets the Inland requirements. But a boat that only complies with the Inland requirements DOES NOT meet the requirements to operate in international waters.

Some states may set forth regulations that pertain ONLY to their state waters. A boat that complies with the state water requirements may not meet the Inland or the International requirements.

Following are the Inland and the International requirements:

Inland —

A. Boats built prior to Dec. 25, 1981, must display lights shown in Fig. 1, Fig. 2 or Fig. 3.
B. Boats built after Dec. 24, 1981, less than 12 meters (approximately 39⅓ feet) in length, must display lights shown in Fig. 1, Fig. 2 or Fig. 3.
C. Boats built after Dec. 24, 1981, 12 meters (approximately 39⅓ feet) or more in length, but less than 20 meters (approximately 65½ feet) in length, must display lights shown in Fig. 1 or Fig. 2.
D. Boats operated on the Great Lakes must display lights shown in Fig. 1 or Fig. 4.

FIGURE 1

FIGURE 2

FIGURE 3   FIGURE 4

International —
  A. Boats less than 20 meters (approximately 65½ feet) in length must display lights shown in Fig. 1 or Fig. 2. If the light arrangement in Fig. 1 is selected, the aft masthead light must be higher than the fore masthead light. If the light arrangement in Fig. 2 is selected, boats less than 12 meters (approximately 39⅓ feet) in length, the masthead light must be one meter (3¼ feet) higher than the port and starboard lights. Boats 12 meters (approximately 39⅓ feet) or more in length, but less than 20 meters (approximately 65½ feet) in length, the masthead light must be 2½ meters (approximately 8-1/6 feet) higher than the gunwale.

  B. Boats less than seven meters (approximately 23 feet) in length and operate at a maximum speed of seven knots (approximately 8 mph) or less, may in place of the light arrangement shown in Fig. 1 or Fig. 2, display one 32 point white light. If practicable, port and starboard lights should be displayed.

  C. Boats operated on the Great Lakes must display lights shown in Fig. 1 or Fig. 4.

Both the Inland and International regulations do not require boats that are less than seven meters (approximately 23 feet) in length to display an anchor light unless anchored in or near a narrow channel, fairway or anchorage, or where other boats normally navigate. But do require any boat that is seven meters (approximately 23 feet) or greater in length, but less than 20 meters (approximately 65½ feet) in length at anchor to display an anchor light. The Inland regulations do not require a boat less than 20 meters (approximately 65½ feet) to display an anchor light when anchored within a special anchorage area designated by the secretary of transportation.

WARNING MARKERS

Areas of the water may be declared restricted or of limited use to boats. It is a good practice to ask local authorities and boating organizations if there are restricted or hazardous areas in the vicinity and how the area is marked. Most areas will be marked using the Uniform State Waterway Marking System which is discussed in the *NAVIGATIONAL AIDS* section. Try to obtain a description of the markers around the restricted area before proceeding towards it.

Boaters must also recognize the two flag designs which indicate that skin divers are present in the area. The flag may be mounted on a buoy or inflated innertube.

When sighting the skin divers flag, slow the boat, look for air bubbles which may indicate the diver is near the boat and steer the boat away from the area. Be prepared to stop quickly.

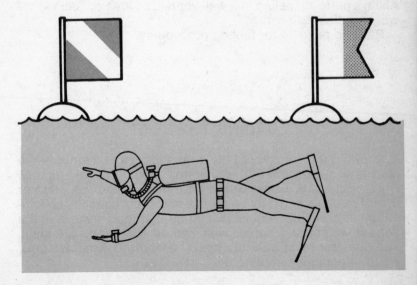

FUELING

Fueling a boat is a very important operation that should be done very carefully. Fuel vapors can be very hazardous if they are not properly and safely dealt with. One cupful of vaporized gasoline has the same explosive power as fifteen sticks of dynamite. Make sure that the ventilation system is always in good and proper operating condition.

⚠WARNING

Gasoline is extremely flammable. DO NOT smoke or allow sparks or open flame around fuel or in presence of fuel vapor. Be sure area is well-ventilated. Observe fire prevention rules.

Before fueling the boat, make sure any match, lighter, cigarette, cigar or pipe is extinguished. To avoid static sparks, the fuel nozzle should contact the fuel tank. Shut off the engine and any other electrical device that could produce a spark. If any fuel spillage occurs, wipe it up immediately. Always perform fueling in a well-ventilated area so fuel vapors will be quickly dispersed.

Refer to page 34 for fueling procedures.

LOADING THE BOAT

Knowing the capacity of the boat and how to distribute the load is a responsibility the operator should not take lightly. Observe the U.S. Coast Guard Maximum Capacities plate or manufacturer's capacity plate. The maximum capacity specification is based upon the assumption that the engine is of the correct weight and horsepower and all conditions are ideal. The operator must alter his load if hazardous wind, water or weather conditions are noted.

U.S. COAST GUARD

MAXIMUM CAPACITIES

13 PERSONS OR 1950 LBS

2430 LBS PERSONS, MOTORS, GEAR
125 H.P. MOTOR

For boats not equipped with a capacity plate, the following formula can be used to determine the number of people you can safely carry under good operating conditions.

$$\text{Number of People} = \frac{\text{Length of Boat X Width of Boat}}{15}$$

Do not measure accessories, only boat hull dimensions. Round the number of people off to the lowest number. Remember it is safer to carry too few people, than to carry too many. This is only an estimate. The formula is based upon the average weight per person onboard is 150 pounds. It also assumes that the engine is of the correct weight and horsepower, there is a normal amount of equipment load onboard and the wind, water and weather conditions are ideal. If excessive equipment load, inclement weather or hazardous water conditions are noted, the operator must alter the number of people as he feels it to be necessary. Always use good and careful judgement. Distribute the load evenly and don't allow people to stand up in small boats.

When climbing onboard a boat, always step in. Never jump into a boat. The operator should board the boat first, making sure all gear is loaded and stowed. Tie down any heavy gear that might slide around. After all gear is secured, have all other people board the boat one at a time dispersing themselves around the boat so that the load is evenly distributed.

VENTILATION

Poor ventilation of fuel vapor is the leading cause of fire and explosion aboard recreational boats. Fuel vapor is heavier than air and will collect in the boat if not ventilated out. A single spark is all that is needed to ignite the fuel vapor.

A ventilation system is required to properly and efficiently ventilate an enclosed engine or fuel compartment. The Federal Law requirements are as follows:

Boats built after April 25, 1940, and prior to August 1, 1980, with engines using gasoline as fuel or any other fuel having a flashpoint of 110°F or less, must be equipped with at least two ventilation ducts (wind scoops). The intake duct must face forward to scoop in the fresh air and the exhaust duct must face aft to expel the collected fuel vapors safely overboard. Flexible tubes at least two inches in diameter must be connected to duct flanges. The intake tube must extend at least halfway to the bilge or at least below the level of the carburetor air intake. The exhaust tube must extend down to the bilge.

On boats built after July 31, 1978, but prior to August 1, 1980, the requirements for ventilation of the fuel tank compartment can be omitted if there is no electrical source of ignition in the fuel tank compartment and if the fuel tank vents to the outside of the boat. After August 1, 1980, all boats with gasoline engines must be built with ventilation systems which comply with the U.S. Coast Guard standards. The operator is required to keep the system in proper operating condition.

This type of ventilation system depends on forward motion of the boat or a good breeze to work properly. If an auxiliary ventilation system with an electric fan is used, make sure fan and fan switch are spark-proof.

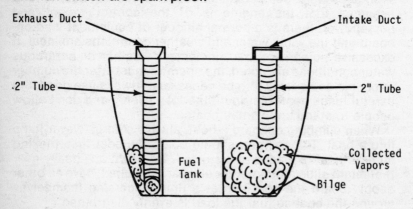

Exhaust Duct   Intake Duct

.2" Tube   2" Tube

Fuel Tank

Collected Vapors

Bilge

FLAME ARRESTER

If a boat built after April 25, 1940 is equipped with a gasoline inboard or inboard-outdrive engine, the carburetor must be fitted with a U.S. Coast Guard approved flame arrester or carry a label indicating that the U.S. Coast Guard has approved the use of the engine without a flame arrester.

Should a carburetor backfire occur, a fire could result if the flame arrester is missing or an unapproved flame arrester is used.

Make sure the flame arrester is free of all foreign matter and all seals are in good condition and fit tight.

An outboard motor is not required to be fitted with a flame arrester.

Flame Arrestor

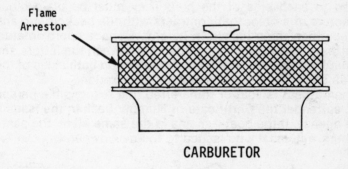

CARBURETOR

SAFETY COURSES

Various organizations offer boating safety courses, some of which are listed under *ORGANIZATIONS* in the back of this manual.

Boat/U.S. Foundation keeps up-to-date records of those safety courses offered by the United States Coast Guard, United States Power Squadrons, American National Red Cross and any state organization that list with them. Toll free number 1-800-336-BOAT can be called anywhere within the United States to provide you with a listing of the safety courses offered in your area.

In addition, check with area marine clubs or organizations and educational institutions for boating safety courses they offer.

LEGAL REQUIREMENTS

NUMBERING

Boat numbering is used for identification purposes. All pleasure boats equipped with machinery propulsion must be numbered. Some states require boats not equipped with machinery propulsion to be numbered, so be sure to check your state boating rules for numbering requirements.

After completion of the state requirements, a Certificate of Number will be issued. The Certificate of Number must be displayed on the boat at all times the boat is in use. On the Certificate of Number will be listed the numbers and letters you must display on each side of the boat's forward half.

The numbers and letters must be painted or permanently attached to each side of the hull. They must be plain block characters of a color that contrasts with the background and not less than three inches in height. A space approximately the size of the letter "M" must be left between the letters and the numbers. Display numbers and letters on both sides of the bow as shown in the accompanying illustration.

When a boat is sold or transferred, the responsible person must surrender the Certificate of Number back to the issuing state agency. If the boat remains in the same state, the same numbers will usually be issued to the new owner.

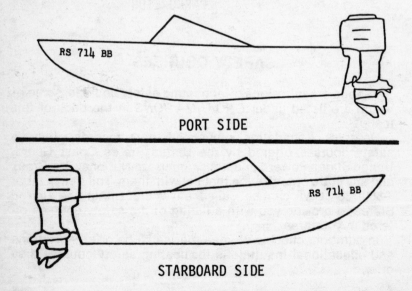

RS 714 BB

PORT SIDE

RS 714 BB

STARBOARD SIDE

EQUIPMENT

Federal law requires that certain minimum equipment be installed on a boat or be carried onboard before it can legally operate on the water. The equipment requirements are dependent upon boat length.

Note that canoes and kayaks are required to carry one personal flotation device (PFD) of any type onboard for each person regardless of boat length. A Type V PFD may be carried in place of any PFD, but only if the Type V PFD is designed for that particular activity in which it is to be used.

A. For a boat less than 16 feet in length, minimum equipment requirements are:
   1. Backfire Flame Arrester—One approved flame arrester on each carburetor of all gasoline engines installed after april 25, 1940, except outboard motors.
   2. Numbering—See previous NUMBERING section.
   3. Ventilation—See requirements listed under VENTILATION on page 28.
   4. Personal Flotation Device (PFD)—Type I, II, III, IV or V for each person onboard.
   5. Sound Signaling Device—Not required, but must be able to produce an efficient sound signal when a hazardous weather or maneuvering situation is encountered.
   6. Fire Extinguisher—When boat is NOT equipped with an approved fixed fire extinguishing system in machinery space or spaces, at least one B-I type approved hand portable fire extinguisher is required. Not required on outboard motorboats if the construction of such motorboat will not permit the entrapment of explosive or flammable gases or vapors.
   7. Pollution Prevention—See *WATER POLLUTION PREVENTION* section.
   8. Visual Distress Signals—See DISTRESS SIGNALS on page 78.
B. For a boat 16 feet or longer but less than 26 feet in length, minimum equipment requirements are:
   1. Backfire Flame Arrester—Same requirements as in Section A.
   2. Numbering—See previous NUMBERING section.
   3. Ventilation—See requirements listed under VENTILATION on page 28.
   4. Personal Flotation Device (PFD)—Type I, II, III or V for each person onboard and one Type IV.

5. Sound Signaling Device—Same requirements as in Section A.
6. Fire Extinguisher—Same requirements as in Section A.
7. Pollution Prevention—See *WATER POLLUTION PREVENTION* section.
8. Visual Distress Signals—See DISTRESS SIGNALS on page 78.

C. For a boat 26 feet or longer but less than 40 feet in length, minimum equipment requirements are:
1. Backfire Flame Arrester—Same requirements as in Section A.
2. Numbering—See previous NUMBERING section.
3. Ventilation—See requirements listed under VENTILATION on page 8.
4. Personal Flotation Device (PFD)—Type I, II, III or V for each person onboard and one Type IV.
5. Sound Signaling Device—Any boat 39'4" (12 meters) or more in length but less than 65'6" (20 meters) must be equipped with a whistle and a bell. The whistle and bell must comply with the specifications listed in Annex 3 of the Inland Navigational Rules Act of 1980. Any boat less than 39'4" carries the same requirements as in Section A.
6. Fire Extinguisher—At least two B-I or one B-II type approved portable fire extinguisher is required. One less B-I type approved portable fire extinguisher is required if an approved fixed fire extinguishing system is used in machinery space or spaces.
7. Pollution Prevention—See *WATER POLLUTION PREVENTION* section.
8. Visual Distress Signals—See DISTRESS SIGNALS on page 78.

D. On a boat 40 feet or longer but not more than 65 feet in length, minimum equipment requirements are:
1. Backfire Flame Arrester—Same requirements as in Section A.
2. Numbering—See previous NUMBERING section.
3. Ventilation—See requirements listed under VENTILATION on page 28.
4. Personal Flotation Device (PFD)—Type I, II, III or V for each person onboard and one Type IV.
5. Sound Signaling Device—Any boat 39'4" (12 meters) or more in length but less than 65'6" (20 meters) must be equipped with a whistle and a bell. The whistle and

bell must comply with the specifications listed in Annex 3 of the Inland Navigational Rules Act of 1980.
6. Fire Extinguisher — At least three B-I or one B-I PLUS one B-II type approved portable fire extinguisher is required. One less B-I type approved portable fire extinguisher is required if an approved fixed fire extinguishing system is used in machinery space or spaces.
7. Pollution Prevention — See *WATER POLLUTION PREVENTION* section.
8. Visual Distress Signals — See DISTRESS SIGNALS on page 78.

AUXILIARY EQUIPMENT

Although auxiliary equipment is not legally required, some equipment should be present onboard as good boating practice and in case you are confronted with an emergency situation. Such items as:

1. Owner's manual
2. Engine service manual
3. Extra key on flotable ring
4. First aid kit
5. Anchor and line
6. Oar or paddle
7. Docking lines and fenders
8. Flashlight
9. Bucket and sponge
10. Hand operated bilge pump
11. Boat hook
12. Towing lines
13. Spare propeller and shear pins
14. Spare drain plugs
15. Navigational aids
16. Spare parts most commonly used
17. Tool kit
18. Rear view mirror for skiing
19. Spare fuel/oil mix
20. Spare engine oil
21. Spare hydraulic fluid
22. Sun protection lotion

OPERATION

FUELING

⚠WARNING

**Gasoline is extremely flammable. DO NOT smoke or
allow sparks or open flame around fuel or in presence of
fuel vapor. Be sure area is well-ventilated. Observe fire
prevention rules.**

Use only the manufacturer's recommended grade of gasoline with the specified octane rating. If the manufacturer's
recommended grade or octane rating of gasoline is not known,
then consult your local dealer or an appropriate maintenance/service manual for the specific recommendation or
recommendations.

Unless the engine manufacturer so specifies, avoid fuels
containing alcohol. Alcohol-blended fuels will cause faster
deterioration of elastomers, e.g., hoses and gaskets. The
water absorbed by the alcohol makes the fuel more corrosive
to metals in the fuel system and engine and may damage fuel
system components.

Most two-stroke outboard motors are lubricated by oil that
is mixed with the fuel. Not all two-stroke oils are suitable for
use in present day outboard motors. Only an oil that is either
produced or recommended by the outboard motor manufacturer, or is BIA certified, should be used.

It is important that the outboard motor manufacturer's
recommended fuel-to-oil ratio be closely followed. Excessive
oil or improper type of oil will cause low power, plug fouling
and excessive carbon build-up. An insufficient amount of oil
will result in inadequate lubrication and rapid internal
damage.

Some later outboard motors are equipped with an oil system
that automatically mixes oil with the fuel at the correct ratio.
An oil reservoir is a part of the oil system and the operator only
needs to maintain the correct oil level in the reservoir. On all
other two-stroke outboard motors, oil is poured into the fuel to
obtain the manufacturer's recommended ratio. Two-stroke oil
should be mixed with the gasoline in a separate container

before pouring the mixture into the motor's fuel tank. Some marinas offer a "premix" which is gasoline already mixed with oil. Before using a "premix" be sure it's satisfactory for your outboard motor.

For a new outboard motor, most manufacturers recommend that extra oil be added during the break-in period and certain steps be followed to increase the motor's longevity and its overall performance potential. If the manufacturer's recommendations are not known, then consult your local dealer or an appropriate maintenance/service manual for the specific recommendations.

Don't cut corners when purchasing fuel or two-stroke oils. The initial savings may be a false economy when you consider the damage poor fuel or unsuitable two-stroke oil can do to your engine.

During each fueling, examine fuel system for signs of leakage or deterioration. If damage is noted, renew or repair component before placing boat back into operation.

Refer to the following precautions when fueling a boat.

1. Always fuel the boat in good light.
2. Fuel up only within a well-ventilated area.
3. Fill all portable tanks on the dock, not in the boat.
4. Use only clean, fresh fuel.
5. Prior to fueling —
   A. Shut off the engine and any other device that could produce a spark.
   B. Extinguish all fires, including pilot lights.
   C. If you are docked, it is a good practice to remove all passengers from the boat.
   D. Close ports, windows, doors and hatches.
   E. Examine the fuel system for leakage or damage.
6. During fueling —
   A. Don't smoke, strike a match or lighter, or operate an electric fan.
   B. Keep the fuel supply nozzle in contact with the fuel tank opening to prevent a static spark.
   C. Wipe up all fuel spills immediately.
7. Keep the fuel tank as full as possible to minimize condensation.
8. Make sure the fuel tank cap fits tightly and the seal is in good condition.
9. After fueling, completely ventilate the boat for at least five minutes or longer if fuel vapors are still smelled.

BOAT LAUNCHING

If "Ramp Courtesy" is exercised by all boaters, everyone will get underway faster and in a more organized manner.

Prepare your boat for launch away from the ramp. Take the time to uncover your boat, raise the lower unit to the up position, install the boat's drain plug, release the tie-downs and if needed, disconnect or remove the trailer stop and directional lights. Store all removed equipment.

Know how to maneuver your rig before attempting launching. It may be embarrassing if your first try at backing is at a public launching ramp.

If possible, look over the launching ramp before launching. Find out if there is anything unusual about the ramp. Even if you have used the launching ramp before, look around to be sure changes have not been made that will affect launching.

Some boaters equip the towing vehicle with a front-mounted trailer hitch. This allows easier manuevering in close quarters, and when used on a rear-wheel-drive towing vehicle, the drive wheels will remain on dry ground.

Before backing the trailer down the ramp, get everybody out of the boat and towing vehicle except the driver. Make sure the winch is in the locked position. If you have a tilt type trailer, make sure the tilt latch is in the locked position and the safety chains are secured.

Back the trailer slowly down the ramp until the stern of the boat is in deep enough water to float when pushed free from the trailer. Try to avoid immersing the trailer hubs in the water.

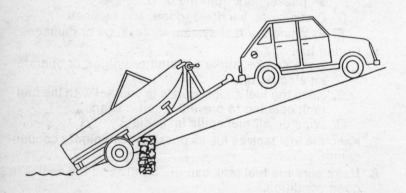

Familiarize yourself with the launch site before attempting to launch the boat.

If it cannot be avoided, at least allow the hubs to cool before submerging them. If this precaution is not observed, the sudden cooling may cause the hub bearings to crack or chip, or draw full of water.

When the trailer is in position for launching the boat, stop the vehicle. Set the emergency brake, but do not turn off the engine. It's a good practice to place a tire stop behind the towing vehicle's tire.

Attach a bow line and hold it. Never cast off all of the lines from the boat before launching.

On tilt type trailers, unlock the tilt latch and release the safety chains. Unlock the winch and release the winch line hook. Shove the boat off the trailer into the water. This is when you will find out if the trailer rollers have been kept properly lubricated. If so, the boat will launch from the trailer easily. Move the towing vehicle and trailer to the parking lot following the launching.

Use the bow line to pull the boat to a dock or boarding platform if one is provided. Secure the boat, then load with all equipment. If no dock or boarding platform is provided, the boat must be boarded over the bow. Hold the bow line ashore until the engine is ready to be started.

Take the time to launch safely, but don't move slowly and lazily when others are waiting to use the ramp.

BOAT RECOVERY

Boat recovery should be performed with the same "Ramp Courtesy" as launching the boat.

To recover the boat, move the boat over to the dock or boarding platform and secure. Remove all of the people onboard and unload all of the equipment. Back the trailer down into position in the same manner as launching.

Using the bow line, maneuver the boat over into position for loading. Raise the lower unit. Unwind the winch line until winch line hook will fasten into bow eye. Winch the boat onto the trailer and secure it. Make sure the winch is in the locked position. If you have a tilt type trailer, make sure the tilt latch is in the locked position and the safety chains are secured.

Move the towing vehicle and trailer with boat to the parking lot area. Remove the drain plug and allow any water to run out. Install tie-downs and if needed, connect or install the trailer stop and directional lights. Make sure all lights operate properly. Complete cleanup and other preparations for towing.

DOCKING AND DEPARTING

Docking or departing, when done well, can be a great ego booster. When done badly, it can result in great embarrassment.

The basic principles behind good docking and departing are the same for most boats, but each boat has its own manuevering characteristics. Only after practicing and experimenting with a boat will you develop the proper handling techniques and feel for the boat. Keep in mind that wind and current will affect manuevering.

Equip your boat with fenders and put them out. Don't risk damaging the exterior of your boat.

DOCKING. To dock the boat, approach the dock slowly and with caution. Note the wind and current; are they from the same or different directions and is either one strong enough to affect boat maneuvering. If the wind and current are parallel to the dock, select the strongest force and maneuver against it, thereby retaining your power and control.

When docking into the wind or current, tie up your bow line first. Securing the stern line first may cause the bow to swing out into the open water.

Docking can be embarrassing.

When docking with the wind or current at your stern, extreme caution must be used. A strong enough wind or current could push you past your docking position. You may need to use slow reverse to hold your position. Tie up your stern line first.

If a strong cross wind or current to the dock is noted, you should start your maneuvering for docking position a little farther away from the dock. The cross wind or current will push your boat towards the dock.

Following is a typical docking procedure. Only after practicing with your boat will you find which type of manuevering works best for your boat under a particular condition.

Approach the dock at a 30°-45° angle from either the port or starboard side. Continue toward the dock while angling the drive unit away from the dock to decrease the approach angle. As docking position nears and boat becomes near parallel to the dock, shift into neutral position. You may need to shift into reverse to stop the boat and angle the drive unit toward the dock to draw the stern of the boat into the dock.

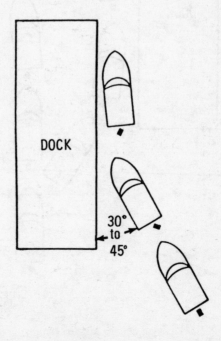

DEPART DOCK. In most cases, it is better to back away from the dock. Forward departure may cause the boat stern to swing into and bump the dock. The following outlines two procedures for departing from the dock.

The first procedure is to angle the drive unit away from the dock. With the engine running, shift the drive unit into reverse and slowly back away from the dock to draw the stern of the boat away from the dock. Continue backwards while gradually straightening the drive unit. When clear of the dock, shift into neutral and angle the drive unit toward the dock to bring the boat parallel with the dock. Angle the drive unit away from the dock and proceed forward.

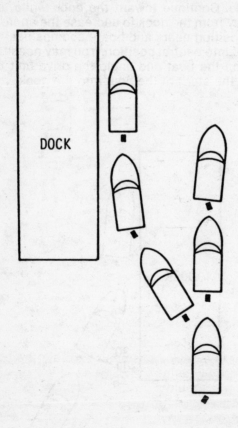

The second procedure is to place the directional **shifter** (gear shift) into neutral position. With the engine running **and** the drive unit facing straight ahead, manually push the boat away from the dock while retaining its parallel position. DO NOT over extend yourself when pushing away from the dock, or you may become an overboard boater. Angle the drive unit away from the dock, shift into forward and proceed slowly.

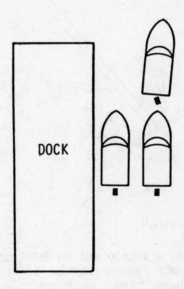

ANCHORING

An anchor is a device designed to retain the boat in a confined area without danger of dragging. The type of anchor and anchor line you should select is based upon:
1. The displacement of your boat.
2. How well your boat resists wind and current drag.
3. The type of bottom you expect to be anchoring in.

The following shows some typical anchoring devices with a brief explanation of each.

Grapnel

Sometimes used on small boats. Originally designed to hook and recover articles lost overboard. Holds best on bottoms covered with coral, rock or grass. Should not be relied upon when anchoring in sand, clay or mud.

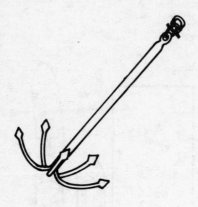

Lightweight Northill

Holding abilities are excellent on most type of bottoms. Some bottom types require special care to set anchor. Anchor's broad flukes have a tendency to ski over bottom's surface.

Danforth

Holding abilities are excellent on most type of bottoms. Some bottom types require special care to set anchor. Anchor's broad flukes have a tendency to ski over bottom's surface.

Mushroom

Smaller sizes are most effective in sand or mud. Larger sizes are often used for permanent moorings.

Plow

Holds best on bottoms covered with mud, sand or shell.

Stockless

Depends mainly on its own weight for holding efficiency. Primarily used aboard larger boats.

A short piece of chain, suitable connectors and an anchor line (rode) is attached to the anchor. The length of chain will improve the anchor's efficiency and will prevent rubbing of the anchor rode on the bottom's surface. Chain weight should be equal to or exceed anchor's weight. Make sure the attaching shackles are as strong as the chain.

Anchor rodes made up of nylon fibers are the most commonly used. The nylon fiber rodes provide strength, elasticity and resistance to moisture and marine life. Anchor rode made of chain is another option.

Use care in selecting an anchoring spot, boats already anchored cannot be expected to move (unless they are in violation). Approach the anchoring spot with the boat's bow into the wind or current, whichever is stronger. Shift into neutral.

Before lowering anchor, make sure anchor rode end is attached to the boat and rode is free of tangles. It is a good practice to attach a buoyed trip line to the crown of the anchor as depicted below. Lower the anchor overboard until it rests on the bottom's surface.

Maintain tension on the rode until sufficient length (scope) has been established. A general rule for anchor rode length is five to seven times the depth of the water. The more hazardous the weather or water conditions, the more the anchor rode length should be increased. Make sure anchor is set before securing anchor rode.

It is not good practice to anchor a boat from the stern. The bow of the boat is designed to ride over the water, while the stern is not.

Find a fixed point on shore and frequently refer to it. This will establish whether or not the anchor is holding.

When releasing the anchor, slowly move towards the top of the anchor while shortening the anchor rode length as you go. Break the anchor loose and retrieve it.

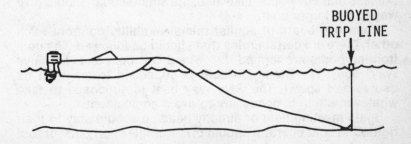

BUOYED TRIP LINE

RULES OF THE ROAD

Most boat operators abide by the "Inland Rules of the Road." The two main purposes of these boat rules are to prevent accidents and to keep everyone underway.

Signals

Like a directional light on an automobile, the whistle or horn on a boat is used as a signaling device. The purpose is to let the other boater know what you are going to do. But, there's no need to blast your whistle or toot your horn at every boat you approach. Use your signaling device only when the situation requires it. When signaling another boater, always give your signal early enough to be noticed and understood.

The signaling code for the length of a whistle blast or toot of a horn is as follows:

Short Blast—about one-second duration
Extended Blast—four-to-six seconds.
Long Blast—eight-to-ten seconds.

The "Inland Rules" danger signal is four or more short blasts or toots. When a boater hears the danger signal, he should slow down or stop and maneuver his boat clear of the confusion or hazardous situation, for example, a boat is backing away from a dock with the operator unaware that there is a boat passing behind him. The operator of the passing boat should give four or more short blasts or toots. The operator of the boat backing away from the dock should come to a stop and take note of the situation.

Rules Of The Road

When two boats of dissimilar maneuverability confront each other, the more maneuverable boat should always give way to the less maneuverable. Likewise, the smaller boat should give way to the larger boat.

When two boats of similar maneuverability confront each other, there are certain rules that should be followed. The confronting boats are termed the "Stand On" boat and the "Give Way" boat. The Stand On boat is supposed to maintain its course and speed. The Give Way boat is supposed to take whatever action is necessary to avoid an accident.

Boats meeting near or directly head-on should stay to their right. One boat operator should give a single short blast or toot and the other operator should respond back with the same signal. Now both operators know what the other one is going to do.

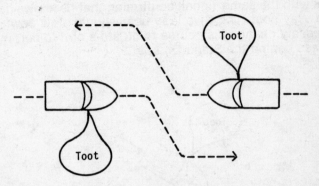

Boats passing starboard-to-starboard should not be a common practice, but changing course in order to pass port-to-port could only create a hazardous situation. Hold your position and give two short blasts or toots. The other operator should respond back with the same signal, confirming your signal has been received and understood.

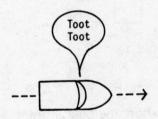

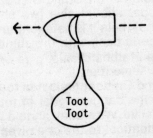

In a crossing situation, the boat on the right has the right-of-way making it the Stand On boat. Although the Inland Rules do not require a signal, the boater on the right should give a single short blast or toot. The other operator should respond back with the same signal, confirming that he knows he is the Give Way boat. The Give Way boat should slow down and if necessary change his course to create a port-to-port meeting or pass behind the Stand On boat.

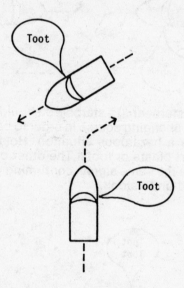

In an overtaking situation, the boat in front is in the Stand On position and the boat behind is in the Give Way position. Under normal circumstances the Give Way boat should pass on the port side of the Stand On boat. To signal his intent, the Give Way boat should give two short blasts or toots. If the Stand On boat feels it is safe for the Give Way boat to pass, he should respond back with the same signal. If the intent is to pass on the starboard side, give one short blast or toot and wait for the same reply.

If the Stand On boat feels it is too dangerous, he should respond with the danger signal of four or more short blasts or toots. The Give Way boat should hold his position until a response, identical to the one given, is received.

The Give Way boat is always the Give Way boat until clearly past the Stand On boat. Pass with caution, don't create a hazardous situation.

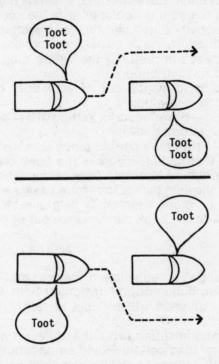

When approaching a blind bend or after backing clear of your dock into a heavily traveled waterway, give one long blast of the horn or whistle.

PERFORMANCE

Poor boat performance might lead a boat owner to think he either bought a lemon or was mislead when he purchased his boat. Assuming the boat is equipped with the correct engine, the engine is properly tuned and the drive system is in good operating condition, the lack of peak performance might be traced to incorrect trim setting, the wrong propeller or improper load and its distribution.

Getting peak performance out of your boat comes with understanding the following:

1. Trim Setting — How does trim setting affect performance and how is it corrected?
2. Propeller — How is the correct propeller selected?
3. Load and Distribution — How is the boat loaded so the load is distributed to obtain peak performance?

Refer to the following paragraphs for a basic explanation of each performance group which may help give you an understanding of how to get peak performance out of your boat.

Trim Setting

The trim setting is an adjustment feature used to compensate for load distribution or hull design, or both. Only a boat that is properly trimmed will be able to reach peak performance.

Only after experimenting with the different trim angles under a particular load condition and its distribution will you find the most efficient and safest riding position.

OUTBOARD MOTORS AND STERN DRIVES. When an outboard or stern drive boat is running at full speed, the propeller shaft should be parallel to the surface of the water. If the boat's bow seems to dig (plow) into the water, either the load distribution is too far forward or the trim angle is too little (lower unit near transom). Make sure the load is evenly distributed, then increase the trim angle to the proper setting. If the boat's bow seems to be too high, either the load distribution is too far aft or the trim angle is too great (lower unit away from transom). Make sure the load is evenly distributed, then decrease the trim angle to the proper setting. Along with poor performance, incorrect trim angle can affect steering proficiency.

Note that the trim angle setting that will offer the best performance under a light load condition, will usually not offer the best performance under a heavy load condition or when pulling water skiers. When pulling a skier with a boat that the ski ropes attach to the stern, the stern is forced down making a decreased trim angle setting more efficient.

INBOARDS AND JET DRIVES. Inboard and jet drive boats are trimmed using devices attached to the boat's hull. Ask your dealer for the correct procedure to adjust the trim properly on your particular boat.

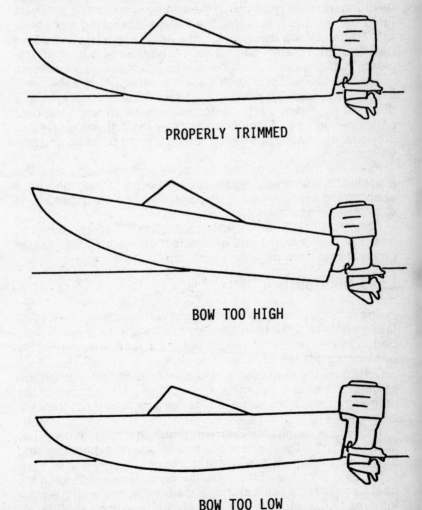

PROPERLY TRIMMED

BOW TOO HIGH

BOW TOO LOW

Propeller Selection

Proper propeller selection is one of the most important factors in your boat and motor reaching a satisfactory performance level. The engine manufacturer or boat builder provides you with a propeller that they have found offers the best overall performance. With the standard propeller and the boat operating at full throttle under a normal load condition, the engine should reach maximum operating rpm range.

A tachometer is a must for determining if the engine is reaching its rated rpm level. If the engine is operating below its rated full throttle rpm range, the engine is laboring and power and efficiency are being lost. If the engine is operating above its rated full throttle rpm range, no additional power or efficiency is being gained and serious engine damage may result.

Special applications such as water skiing, high speed performance or carrying a heavy load may require a propeller of a different diameter, pitch, design or material to reach the best performance level. Some boaters carry more than one type of propeller so boat performance can be altered by swapping propellers.

Keep the boat hull bottom and drive unit housing clean. If a propeller is damaged, repair should be performed only in a shop that is experienced in propeller restoration. If damage is excessive, renew propeller.

Refer to *PROPELLER* section for a basic understanding of how a propeller works and what effect diameter, pitch, design and material have on how it performs.

Load Distribution

The distribution of onboard weight will have a noticeable effect on how well the boat handles and its ability to reach peak performance. Too much weight will make it difficult or near impossible to get the boat up on a plane.

Distribute the load evenly. Improper fore and aft distribution of weight affects the planing angle of the boat or thrust of the propeller in much the same manner as a drive unit not trimmed correctly.

Too much weight forward will make the boat "plow." Too much weight aft will cause the boat's bow to bounce up and down in a patterned movement (porpoise).

For best overall performance, the general rule is to keep the boat as parallel to the water as possible. On boats with a planing type hull, distribute the load so the bow rises slightly.

PROPELLERS

A propeller is designed to move a boat through the water in somewhat the same manner that a wood screw passes through a piece of wood. Propellers are rated by diameter, pitch and the number of blades. Diameter is the distance across a circle described by the blade tips and pitch is the forward thrust imparted in one revolution of the propeller.

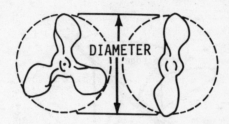

The correct propeller diameter is determined by motor design, especially the items of horsepower and propeller shaft gear ratio, and should usually not be changed from that recommended by the manufacturer. Propeller pitch is more nearly comparable to the transmission gear ratio of an automobile and should be individually selected to suit the conditions of boat design and usage. Propeller blade number affects efficiency and vibration level. The lower the blade number, the higher the efficiency and the higher the vibration. Because of this, most propellers are made with three blades. The efficiency difference between two- and three-blade propellers is thought not to be as important as the vibrational difference.

Efficiency is greatest when the propeller operates with minimal slippage. Slippage is the difference between the distance a boat actually moves forward with each turn of the propeller and the theoretical distance indicated by the pitch. For example, a boat equipped with a 12-inch pitch propeller which moves forward nine inches with each revolution of the propeller shaft has 25% slippage. Actual amount of accepted slippage is usually dependent upon the type of application. Normal slippage on a racing hull may be as low as 10%, while a slow speed hull may normally be allowed 50-60%.

With the wide range of propeller applications, various propeller types and propeller design features are used to provide the best performance for the intended application. The following describes some propeller types and various design features.

A constant pitch (flat blade) propeller operates efficiently only at relatively slow rotative speeds. Above a certain critical speed, water is moved from the blade area faster than additional water can flow into the area behind the blades, causing "cavitation" and erratic behavior. The extreme turbulence and shock waves caused by cavitation rapidly reduces operating efficiency.

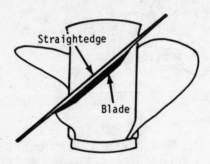

CONSTANT PITCH

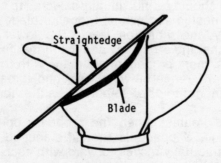

PROGRESSIVE PITCH

The progressive pitch propeller has an assigned pitch number that is the average pitch over the entire blade length. The propeller is designed to improve performance at higher speeds or when the propeller breaks the water surface.

A cupped propeller is a propeller that has the trailing edge of the blades curled outward from the boat. The cupped blades help the propeller to hold water better when operating in a cavitating or ventilating condition (ventilation is defined in a later paragraph). This will allow the engine or drive unit to be further adjusted for optimum performance. Cupping will normally add one-half inch to one inch of pitch, which will usually cause engine full throttle rpm to be reduced by 150-300 rpm. Cupping usually has no benefit on propellers that are used in applications of heavy duty work or when the propeller always remains fully submerged.

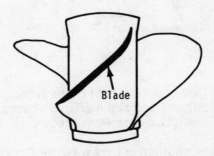

CUPPED BLADE

Blade rake is the amount the blade slants back towards the aft end of the propeller. Most standard propellers are raked from 0-20 degrees. Generally the higher rake angle will improve the ability of the propeller to operate in a cavitating or ventilating condition.

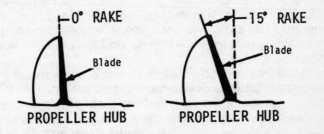

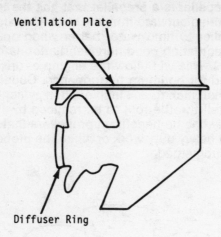

Ventilation Plate

Diffuser Ring

On models that expel exhaust through the propeller hub, a diffuser ring is often used at the aft end of the propeller hub to help prevent exhaust gases from feeding back into the propeller blades.

A ventilation condition occurs when air from the water's surface or engine exhaust outlet is sucked into the tips of the propeller blades reducing normal water load, thereby causing the engine to momentarily overspeed. The excessive rpm may cause cavitation, further reducing forward thrust. Usually an anti-ventilation plate is cast into the drive unit lower housing (directly above the propeller) to eliminate or reduce the possibility of air being sucked in.

Propellers are usually constructed of aluminum, bronze, plastic or stainless steel. Aluminum propellers are most commonly used on outboards and stern drives. Bronze propellers are commonly used on inboard applications. Plastic propellers are primarily used on low horsepower engine applications. Stainless steel propellers are popular on high performance applications.

NOTE: It is not a good practice to use bronze propellers in salt water applications due to galvanic corrosion.

Select a propeller or propellers that fits your needs. Remember it is extremely important that the engine reaches manufacturer's rated rpm at full throttle operation. Only then will you get optimum performance out of your engine. Use a good-quality tachometer to measure rpm and replace your propeller if needed. Note the following list of some important points to remember:

1. Insufficient pitch will cause engine to overspeed.
2. Too much pitch will cause engine to "lug" and not reach recommended rpm level.
3. When water skiing or carrying a heavy load, an adjustment to a lower pitch propeller may be required.
4. A low pitched propeller will usually allow the boat to get on plane quicker, but reduced top speed, poor fuel economy and accelerated engine wear could result.

REMOVE AND INSTALL PROPELLER

There are two general methods of transferring power from the propeller shaft to the propeller. One method uses splines on the propeller shaft and propeller hub, while the other method uses a pin (commonly called a shear pin) that passes through the propeller shaft and propeller hub.

⚠WARNING

Be sure ignition is "OFF" and gear selector is in "NEUTRAL" when servicing propeller, otherwise, accidental starting can occur if propeller shaft is rotated.

Splined Type

Propellers which have a splined hub also have a rubber cushion ring that surrounds the hub and absorbs shock should the propeller strike an obstruction. This type propeller is held on the propeller shaft by a nut. Unscrew the nut then slide the propeller off the shaft to remove the propeller. Don't lose any washers or spacers which may also be found on the shaft.

In some instances, the nut may be rusty or extremely tight. Apply a lubricating solvent to shaft threads to loosen rust. If needed, a block of wood may be positioned between the propeller and the anti-ventilation plate to prevent propeller rotation while unscrewing the nut.

Before installing the propeller, liberally coat the propeller shaft splines and threads with a water-resistant grease. Be sure you correctly install all spacers and washers. Tighten the propeller nut securely. There should be no fore-aft movement

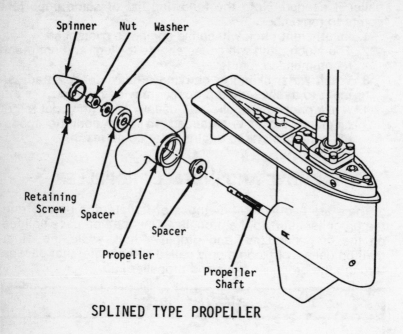

Spinner   Nut   Washer

Retaining
Screw   Spacer

Spacer

Propeller

Propeller
Shaft

SPLINED TYPE PROPELLER

of propeller after tightening nut; if there is movement, something is worn or missing and must be corrected. The nut should be locked in place after tightening with a cotter pin or by bending the tab on the tab washer, depending on the type of locking method used.

Shear Pin Type

Removal of propellers using the shear pin arrangement should be evident after inspection. Note that many units are equipped with a spinner attached to the end of the propeller. The spinner should unscrew after removing the cotter pin.

Shear pins are designed to break if the propeller strikes an obstruction thereby protecting the drive unit. Shear pins are made of a metal specified by the outboard motor or stern drive manufacturer. Except in an emergency, use only the size and type shear pin specified by the manufacturer; DO NOT substitute.

It is a good practice to carry several shear pins and cotter pins that fit your unit.

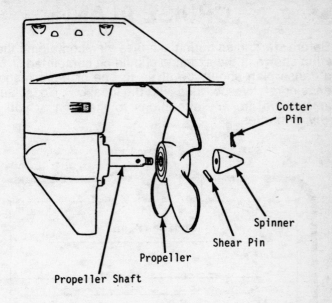

Cotter
Pin

Spinner

Shear Pin

Propeller

Propeller Shaft

SHEAR PIN TYPE PROPELLER

CRUISE PLAN

Before starting an outing, a cruise plan containing the information shown in the example should be completed. A copy of the cruise plan should be given to one or more responsible friends or relatives, or filed with the local U.S. Coast Guard office. If there are any alterations to the plan or you return, notify all parties.

Cruise Plan

Boater's Identification:

Name_____ Phone No._____

Address_____

Boat Identification:

Registration No._____ Make/Model_____

Hull Color_____ Interior Color_____

Overall Length_____ Power Type_____

Data:

Number of Persons on Board_____

Departure, Date_____ Time_____

   Location_____ Destination_____

Route/Time of Travel_____

Return Departure, Date_____ Time_____

Will Return No Later Than, Date_____ Time_____

Radio (Yes/No)_____ Freqs._____

Trailer License No._____

Automobile, Make/Model_____ Color_____

   License No._____ Parked At_____

Other Information_____

Important Telephone Numbers:

U.S. Coast Guard_____

Local Authority_____

Other_____

UNITED STATES COAST GUARD

Operating as a branch of the U.S. armed forces, the Coast Guard is the federal government's primary marine law enforcement agency. The Coast Guard operates under the control of the Department of Transportation during peacetime or, in time of war or upon presidential order, as a part of the Department of the Navy.

The Coast Guard regulates vessels, sets and enforces safety standards and dictates license requirements for merchant seamen. These standards apply to vessels constructed in or under the control of the United States.

Units within the Coast Guard propose regulations to the Marine Safety Council, which is comprised of the Coast Guard's chief counsel and heads of six other Coast Guard offices. The council ratifies or rejects any proposed regulations.

Coast Guard boats are identified by the words "Coast Guard" down the side, distinctive stripes, U.S. Coast Guard Ensign and uniformed personnel.

The Coast Guard has the authority to impose fines and to terminate the use of an unsafe boat. The Coast Guard requires that specified, approved safety equipment is onboard, that the boat is in safe operational condition and that the boat is operated safely. Failure to do so may result in a civil or criminal offense.

If you are instructed by Coast Guard personnel to stop, **STOP IMMEDIATELY.** Maneuver your boat to allow boarding. Remember, like an onshore officer, the Coast Guard personnel are out there for a purpose, **SAFE BOATING.** Treat them with respect; they may save your life someday.

NAVIGATIONAL AIDS

COMPASS

The most valuable navigational aid, particularly when you are lost, is a compass. Even a crude compass can assist in determining the direction to shore when visual sighting is not possible. A compass should be found on any boat operated on large bodies of open water or where the possibility of foul weather may cause disorientation.

The compass may be hand-held or permanently fixed as a part of the boat's instrumentation. To be useful as a navigational aid, the compass must be marked in degrees and some form of sighting mechanism should be provided, otherwise directional accuracy will be marginal.

Desired accuracy when using a compass is determined by the situation. The accuracy required to find a point on a small lake's shoreline may be significantly less than the accuracy required to plot a course over a large expanse of water. If instruction in compass reading is desired, contact a boating organization or club in your area.

Special mention should be made that when using a compass it must be located away from objects that will affect the compass reading, such as motors and electrical devices.

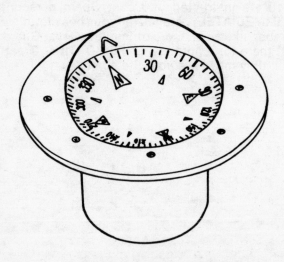

TYPICAL MARINE COMPASS

NAUTICAL CHARTS

Nautical charts are advisable and may be necessary if you intend to travel in waters you are unfamiliar with. And even though you may have traveled the same waterway a number of times, a chart of the area may prove interesting and informational.

Nautical charts will display such information as water depth, obstructions, restricted areas and shoreline features. A mileage scale will be provided as well as a compass rose to determine headings. The nautical chart is essential when planning a long voyage over unfamiliar water where distance and compass headings are required. An up-to-date chart should be used when undertaking a voyage to prevent surprises which may be found when using an old chart, particularly if the waterway is well-traveled or subject to construction activity.

It is a good practice to obtain charts before starting a trip rather than waiting until you arrive in an area to try and locate a chart. Local supplies of charts may be depleted particularly at the beginning of the boating season. If you can, obtain all charts before you leave so you don't waste time later in the trip.

Protect the chart you're using when navigating by enclosing it in a clear plastic case or cover. If the cover is clear on both sides, then two charts can be inserted back-to-back. The cover is then just flipped over to read the other chart. If the cover is constructed of hard plastic it is less likely to be blown about by the wind.

Nautical charts are produced by various government agencies which have responsibility for certain areas. Consult your marine dealer to determine which agency provides charts for a certain waterway, or contact the Coast Guard.

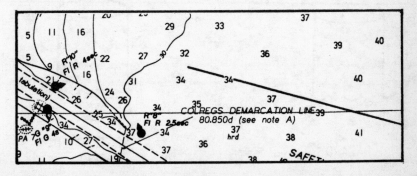

WATERWAY MARKING SYSTEMS

Just as roads and highways are marked to provide information and regulate traffic flow, waterways are marked to provide navigational assistance and warn of hazards. Two major marking systems are used in the United States. They are the Uniform State Waterway Marking System and the Lateral Marking System.

Certain precautions must be followed when boating near navigational markers. Navigational aids and warning devices are protected by law. Destruction, defacement, obstruction or any action which may affect the proper operation of a navigational aid is a criminal offense. If you should accidentally collide with a marker, or if you believe an aid is mislocated or operating improperly, contact the responsible authority.

Uniform State Waterway Marking System

The Uniform State Waterway Marking System (USWMS) was devised to provide a uniform marking system for marking inland streams and lakes under state jurisdiction. This system is common to most states and may be used in your area.

The USWMS uses two classes of markers, regulatory and navigation.

The regulatory markers or buoys are white with two orange bands and have an information symbol located between the orange bands. An open diamond symbol indicates there is a hazard to be avoided, while a diamond with crossed lines indicates an area that is closed or restricted to boats.

HAZARD

RESTRICTED
AREA

A regulatory buoy with a circle provides control information such as a speed limit.

CONTROL
BUOY

Information contained in a box is usually piloting information.

INFORMATION
BUOY

Regulatory information may also appear on shoreline markers.

Navigation buoys are usually colored black or red to mark the limits of the channel. When used in pairs the boat should be steered between the paired buoys to follow a safe course.

CHANNEL
LIES
BETWEEN
BUOYS

Navigation buoys that are white with a red or black top are used to direct boats away from hazardous sections. If the white buoy has a red top then the boat should pass to the south or west of the buoy. If the white buoy has a black top then the boat should pass to the north or east of the buoy.

PASS TO
NORTH OR
EAST

PASS TO
SOUTH OR
WEST

A buoy marked with red and white vertical stripes indicates a hazardous area between the buoy and shore. Pass the buoy on the open water side.

HAZARD BETWEEN
BUOY AND SHORE

Lateral Marking System

The Lateral Marking System is used in coastal areas and on large waterways where the Coast Guard is responsible for navigational aids. The Lateral system provides more information and is more sophisticated than the previously discussed USWMS system. The Lateral system is currently being modified to coincide with an international buoyage system. Modification will be accomplished during normal maintenance of the Lateral system until 1989 when all changes should be completed. Differences between the new and old systems will be noted in the following discussion.

The Lateral system displays information on buoys and signs known as daymarkers. Daymarkers are square or triangular shaped signs that are attached to posts driven into the bottom of the waterway. Daymarkers are generally used in shallow water where a buoy is not required.

NOTE: When using the Lateral system, the starboard and port sides of the channel are as viewed when entering the channel from the direction of the sea, when going upstream on rivers, or when going from a lake's outlet to its upper end.

BUOYS. Port and starboard channel marking buoys are differentiated by their color, shape and number. Port side buoys are green (new system) or black (old system), cylindrical and numbered with odd numbers. Because port buoys are cylindrical from top to bottom they are termed "can" buoys. Starboard side buoys are red, cone shaped at the top and numbered with even numbers. Starboard buoys are termed "nun" buoys because of their cone-shaped top.

CAN BUOY

NUN BUOY

Buoys are numbered in ascending order from the beginning of the channel with odd numbered buoys to port and even numbered buoys to starboard.

Buoys marked with a contrasting band of color indicate that the channel splits. If the buoy is a can with a red band, then the preferred channel is to the starboard side of the buoy. If the buoy is a nun with a green (new system) or black (old system) band, then the preferred channel is to the port side of the buoy.

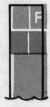

PREFERRED
CHANNEL

TO STARBOARD   TO PORT

Buoys may be equipped with a signal device such as a light, bell, gong or whistle. These buoys are colored and marked the same as the previously discussed unlighted buoys. Note, however, that the nun buoy (cone shaped) exists only as an unlighted buoy. All lighted buoys are cylindrical but the markings provide the same information as the markings on the unlighted buoys. Under the old system a white light was mounted on buoys marking channel sides, while under the new system a green light is mounted on green buoys (port) and a red light is mounted on red buoys (starboard).

CHANNEL SIDE

PORT   STARBOARD

Buoys are also used to indicate mid-channel or safe water. The buoy is either the cylinder type or spherical. The buoy is colored with red and white vertical panels under the new system, while black and white panels were used under the old system. A white light is mounted on lighted buoys and a red sphere is positioned above the light. Cylinder buoys may be equipped with a sounding device.

MID-CHANNEL BUOYS

DAYMARKERS. Daymarkers are colored and numbered the same as buoys. Green, square daymarkers with odd numbers denote the port side of the channel, while red, triangular daymarkers with even numbers denote the starboard side of the channel.

CHANNEL SIDE

PORT   **STARBOARD**

Preferred channel daymarkers display a contrasting color band. Square markers with a red band indicate the preferred channel is to starboard of the marker. Triangular markers with a green band indicate the preferred channel is to port of the marker.

PREFERRED
CHANNEL

TO STARBOARD   TO PORT

Daymarkers which indicate mid-channel or safe channel are red and white and have an octagonal shape.

MID-CHANNEL

CHART SYMBOLS. Buoys and markers of the Lateral system are indicated on nautical charts. If the buoy is equipped with a sound device, the chart will name the type. The chart will list the symbols used to denote buoys and markers on the chart.

Intercoastal Waterway System

The Intercoastal Waterway is marked with navigational aids. The marking system is the same as the Lateral system except there is a yellow band around the bottom of the buoy.

WEATHER

A safety-minded boater is observant of present and future weather conditions. Even if the present weather conditions are clear skies and smooth waters, the boat operator should know the weather forecast and if bad weather is forecast, when it is expected to develop.

Forecast services include: U.S. Coast Guard weather broadcasts, 2670 kHz (VHF/FM); U.S. Weather Service broadcasts, 162.55 MHz or 162.40 MHz (VHF/FM); local radio and TV stations; telephone calls to the closest marina, yacht club, local or state police, marine patrol, U.S. Coast Guard or U.S. Weather Service.

When a reliable weather forecast is not available, good judgement by the operator must be exercised. Only after deciding that weather conditions are suitable, and will be suitable for safe operation for the duration of the trip, should a trip be started.

Special day and night signaling devices are used to warn boaters of weather danger. Many marinas, launching ramps, yacht clubs and U.S. Coast Guard stations display a daytime warning flag or flags and a nighttime warning light or lights. Refer to the following WARNING SIGNALS for weather danger displays.

WARNING SIGNALS

Warning signals displayed by many marinas, launching ramps, yacht clubs and U.S. Coast Guard stations are used to advise boaters of dangerous weather conditions. When a warning signal is displayed, don't ignore it. Weather conditions can be very unpredictable. A light thunderstorm or mild breeze could turn into a very dangerous condition for a small boat.

Learn the meanings of the daytime danger flags and the nighttime danger lights on the following page.

If you are a small boat operator, don't ignore a "Small Craft Warning." Be a safety-minded operator, stay ashore or go to the nearest shore. Securely tie up the boat and if possible cover all boat openings making sure the cover is tightly fastened.

SMALL CRAFT	GALE	STORM	HURRICANE
Winds up to 38 mph	Winds up to 54 mph	Winds up to 72 mph	Winds 72 mph and up

	SMALL CRAFT	GALE	STORM	HURRICANE
DAYTIME SIGNALS				
NIGHT TIME SIGNALS				

WARNING SIGNALS

RADIO EQUIPMENT

Smaller boats used for recreation or fishing are not required by the Federal Communications Commission (FCC) to be equipped with a radio station. A boater may voluntarily equip his boat, but he must possess both a Ship Station License and at least a Restricted Radiotelephone Operators Permit (RP) before he can operate his radio. All marine radio users are responsible for observing both FCC and U.S. Coast Guard regulations.

To apply for a Ship Station License or Restricted Radiotelephone Operator Permit (RP), write to: FCC, P.O. Box 1040, Gettysburg, PA 17325. For additional marine radio information, write to: FCC, 1919 M Street NW, Washington DC 20554 or refer to your area telephone directory for the FCC field office nearest you.

On all boats not equipped with a marine radio, a portable radio capable of receiving the latest official weather forecast should be used.

WATER SKIING SAFETY AND SIGNALS

Water skiing is a very physical and challenging sport that can be very pleasureable if certain safety precautions are observed. Following is a list of safety ideas that may help to reduce water skiing accidents.

1. Make sure all equipment is in good operational condition.
2. Know the waters you are skiing in. Take a trial run of the intended skiing route and look for any underwater hazards.
3. Don't ski near swimmers or in an area that is heavily congested with boats.
4. A person unable to swim should not be allowed to ski.
5. Make sure a proper Personal Flotation Device (PFD) is worn. A PFD designed for water skiing provides more comfort and freedom of movement.
6. Don't pull a skier any faster than he is comfortable going.
7. Carry a second person onboard as an observer. The boat operator must be free to pay full attention to the boats and waters ahead and around him.
8. A fallen skier should be given immediate attention.
9. Stop the engine when nearing a fallen skier for pickup. It is good practice to pick up a skier on the side of the boat that is shielded from the wind.
10. Pay attention to the location of the ski rope or ropes. Don't allow the rope to become tangled in the propeller.

The American Water Skiing Association (AWSA) has designed a set of hand signals they recommend the skier, observer and boat operator know and use.

SPEED SLOWER   STOP

SKIER'S OK SIGNAL   BACK TO DOCK

SPEED FASTER   SPEED OK

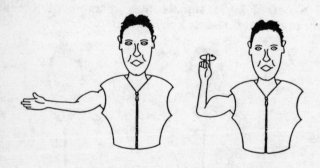

RIGHT TURN   CIRCLE

CUT MOTOR   LEFT TURN

SKIER IN WATER

ACCIDENTS

Accident reports must be filed within the state the accident occurred. Report forms are available through a state agency or U.S. Coast Guard office. Federal law requires the operator to file an accident report if the accident involves a recreational boat, its equipment or any boat required to be legally numbered if any one of the following conditions occur:

1. A human death results from the accident.
2. An injured person requires medical attention beyond first aid.
3. Damage to boat or property is $200 or more, or a complete loss of a boat.
4. A person disappears from a boat under circumstances that indicate death or injury.

If the operator is unable to file a report, all people onboard should file a report or appoint a person to file the report.

If a person dies within 24 hours of the accident or requires medical attention beyond first aid, a report must be filed within 48 hours of the accident.

If an accident only involves a boat or its equipment, a report must be filed within 10 days if the damage is $200 or more.

If an accident occurs, consult the state laws. Some states require accident reports for less serious accidents.

WATER POLLUTION PREVENTION

The Refuse Act of 1899 prohibits the throwing, discharging or depositing of any kind of refuse matter into the waters of the United States, including water from the coastline to three miles out.

The Federal Water Pollution Control Act prohibits the discharging of oil or hazardous substances into the waters as outlined within the act. Federal regulations issued under the Federal Water Pollution Control Act should be consulted. Contact your local U.S. Coast Guard office.

All recreational boats with installed toilet facilities must have an installed, operable Marine Sanitation Device (MSD). Boats 65 feet in length and under may use a U.S. Coast Guard certified MSD of the Type I, II or III. All U.S. Coast Guard certified MSDs are so labeled, except for some holding tanks which are automatically certified under the regulations if they only store sewage and flushwater at ambient air pressure and temperature.

DON'T POLLUTE!

EMERGENCIES

Should an emergency develop, knowing and executing the correct emergency procedure could keep you afloat, allow you to make an emergency repair, bring needed help or save a person's life. Don't ignore your responsibilities as a boat operator. Carry the needed emergency equipment and know how to use it. During an emergency, proceed calmly and methodically and use good common sense.

FIRST AID

Because boats usually operate in areas where professional medical assistance is not readily available, a boat operator should become familiar with basic first aid procedures. An operator should be able to care for himself and the people onboard the boat in the event of an accident or unexpected illness.

Literature on emergency first aid procedures as well as training classes are offered through most Red Cross chapters. Contact your local Red Cross chapter or write to the American National Red Cross, 17th & D Streets N.W., Washington, D.C. 20006.

First aid courses may also be offered by an area hospital, health clinic, school or other organization.

VISUAL DISTRESS SIGNALS

During an emergency, any signal that will attract attention and bring needed help is all right. But displaying a recognized distress signal increases your chances of receiving help.

A universally recognized distress signal that does not require any equipment is to slowly and repeatedly raise and lower your outstretched arms.

Equipment type visual distress signals, at this time, are not required to be carried on all recreational boats. But because they are universally recognized distress signals, it is considered a good boating practice to carry them onboard.

Federal regulation requires all recreational boats as of January 1, 1981, to carry onboard equipment type visual distress signals when used on coastal waters (which includes the Great Lakes, the territorial seas and those waters directly connected to the Great Lakes and the territorial seas, up to a point where the waters are less than two miles wide) and boats owned in the United States when operating on the high seas.

Exceptions are (sunrise to sunset only):
1. Recreational boats less than 16 feet in length.
2. Boats participating in organized events such as races, regattas or marine parades.
3. Open sailboats not equipped with propulsion machinery and less than 26 feet in length.
4. Manually propelled boats.

Equipment type visual distress signals are either pyrotechnic (firework type) or non-pyrotechnic.

Pyrotechnic type signals must be U.S. Coast Guard approved, in serviceable condition (serviceable life date must not be passed and date cannot exceed 42 months from the date of manufacture) and stowed to be readily accessible. Signal launchers produced before January 1, 1981, are not required to be U.S. Coast Guard approved.

NOTE: Launchers may be considered a firearm in some states. State authority should be consulted before launcher is acquired.

Pyrotechnic devices are:
1. Hand-held or aerial red flares.
2. Hand-held or floating orange smoke.
3. Hand-held or launched aerial red meteors or parachute flares.

Federal law requires that if pyrotechnic signaling devices are used, a minimum of three must be carried. If day signaling devices are required, a combination of three daytime and three nighttime signaling devices may be used or three day/night signaling devices meet both requirements. If only night signaling devices are required, either three night signaling devices or three day/night signaling devices meet requirements.

Non-pyrotechnic type signals must carry the manufacturer's certification that they meet U.S. Coast Guard requirements. They also must be in serviceable condition and stowed to be readily accessible.

Non-pyrotechnic devices are:
1. Orange distress flag (day use only).
2. Electric distress light (night use only).

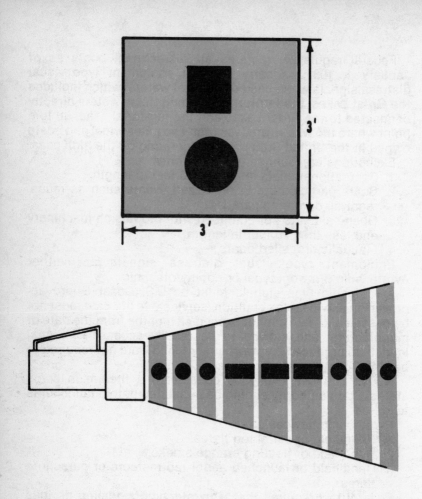

The distress flag must be at least 3' x 3' with a black square and ball on an orange background. The electric distress light must automatically flash the international "SOS" distress signal, which is: three shorts, three longs, three shorts (. . . − − − . . .). A distress light must be capable of flashing a signal four to six times each minute. Note that an ordinary flashlight is not acceptable since it must be manually operated to produce the proper signal and it normally does not produce sufficient candlepower.

Federal law requires that if non-pyrotechnic signaling devices are used, both a distress flag and a distress light must be carried to comply with both daytime and nighttime requirements. If only a night signaling device is required, an electric distress light meets the requirement.

Choose your distress signaling devices with care, some devices work better in a particular weather condition than others. Carrying several different types is considered a good practice.

Make sure pyrotechnic devices are stowed in a cool, dry location and are properly packed. A good practice is to store pyrotechnic signaling devices in a watertight container painted red or orange and identified with the marking "DISTRESS SIGNALS."

⚠WARNING

Pyrotechnic signaling devices can cause injury and property damage if not handled or used properly. Follow manufacturer's directions. Stow pyrotechnic devices so they are inaccessible to children.

RADIO
DISTRESS SIGNALS

A VHF marine radio is probably the best device for calling for help as the VHF marine radio channels are a primary communication system for marine use. The radio telephone distress and calling frequencies 2182 kHz and 156.8 MHz (channel 16) are monitored by U.S. Coast Guard stations, boating agencies, boats and marine facilities.

A CB radio should be considered mainly for personal communication needs. Although CB channel 9 is now monitored by the U.S. Coast Guard Search and Rescue Stations and other volunteer organizations, CB radio should not be considered an adequate substitute for a VHF marine radio.

Listed below are three international emergency signals. If a routine message is interrupted by any one of these three distress signals, priority must be given to the distress message.

1. MAYDAY—to request immediate assistance when threatened with a life or death situation.
2. PAN PAN—used when the safety of the boat or a person is in jeopardy.
3. SECURITY—used for navigation and weather warnings.

EMERGENCY PROCEDURES

If you are confronted with an emergency situation, knowing how you should act and being prepared to act in the correct manner are the first steps toward properly handling an emergency.

Review the following emergency procedures for an explanation of the accepted practices.

Fire Afloat

Being onboard a boat when a fire occurs can be a very scary experience. Remaining calm and handling the fire in a rational manner is very important.

If the boat is in operation when the fire occurs, stop the boat. Position the boat so the fire is downwind; e.g., if the fire is in the bow of the boat, turn the boat's stern into the wind. If the fire is in the aft end of the boat, turn the boat's bow into the wind.

If the fire is burning ordinary combustible materials such as wood, cloth or paper, extinguish the fire using a Class A fire extinguisher or water. You might also attempt to carefully throw the burning material overboard into the water. If the fire burns flammable liquid, oil or grease, then a fire extinguisher must be used to put out the fire. Aim the extinguisher nozzle at the base of the flames, then operate the extinguisher until the fire is completely extinguished.

Be extremely careful if there is the possibility of an explosion. You may need to abandon the boat. Fit everyone with the

correct PFD before entering the water. Stay clear of the boat and position everyone in a group.

Lost

Becoming confused or losing your bearings while on water is not a pleasant feeling. But if you remain calm and methodically trace your steps, chances are you will find your way back on the correct course.

Before starting an outing, chart the course you plan on taking. So, if you should become lost you can systematically trace your steps or convey to another party your intended course.

If you become lost when there is still daylight and visibility is still good, consult your nautical chart or look for a marina, U.S. Coast Guard boat, local water patrol boat or other boaters who might be able to assist you.

If you become lost in a heavy fog or darkness, it is sometimes best to anchor your boat and stay where you are until there is sufficient visibility to continue. If the water is too deep for a bottom anchor, make a sea anchor by using your bailing bucket or empty fuel can and filling it full of water. Use a rope or tie the sea anchor to the boat's bow. Turn on your anchor light.

If you are anchored in a heavy fog, use your sound signaling device to warn other boaters of your location. Recognized fog signals are an extended blast (four-to-six seconds) of your horn or ringing your bell for not longer than one minute.

Boater Overboard

In the majority of cases, a boater falling overboard is a result of unsafe boating practices. The boat operator is responsible for the safety of all boaters onboard and the operator should require that all persons follow safe practices.

Falling overboard often occurs when a person is boarding a small boat and the person loses balance as a result of the unstable footing. People should be assisted in boarding if there is a possibility of falling overboard.

While onboard, all people should be sitting or have access to a secure hand-hold.

While underway, the boat operator must avoid maneuvers which may pitch someone overboard.

Should a person fall overboard, you should use one of two methods for recovery. The first method is self-rescue. With this method you allow the person overboard to rescue himself. As long as the overboard person is not injured, unconscious or in a panicked condition, self-rescue is the preferred method. When you see a person go overboard and he is near the boat, stop the boat immediately and turn off the engine. Get some type of flotation device out to him immediately, even if it is not the correct PFD. This will buy you some time and allow you to get the correct PFD out to him. Allow him to swim to the boat, while keeping verbal contact. If there is considerable distance between the boat and the overboard person, maneuver the boat near the overboard person before proceeding as outlined earlier.

If the overboard person is injured, unconscious or in a panicked condition, the second rescue method must be used. Maneuver the boat upwind from the overboard person with the operator's side of the boat facing the overboard person, then turn off the engine. If the overboard person is able to grasp, throw him a line and pull him alongside the boat. If not, allow the boat to drift towards him, then use whatever method is needed to recover him. Be careful not to cause any further injury.

NOTE: Put a rescuer in the water only as a last resort. Having to save two people is twice as hard as saving one. Make sure the rescuer wears the correct PFD before entering the water.

Capsizing

In most cases, a boat overturns due to unsafe operation, overloading or poor load distribution. Know the load capacity of your boat and evenly distribute the load.

Most pleasure boats will not sink right away, if at all. Sufficient flotation is usually built into the boat so the boat will float even when upright and full of water. In some cases, smaller boats that overturn may be turned upright.

If your boat capsizes, get everyone (if possible) into the correct PFD. Stay with the boat as it will be more easily spotted. Only swim to shore after calmly evaluating the situation and distance. Distance is sometimes longer than first conceived.

Disabled

When a boat is disabled, it is usually due to a problem with the fuel system, ignition system or drive unit. In most cases the problem is minor and can be found and repaired by using good common sense.

You should have onboard a selection of tools that will enable you to perform simple repairs. You should also stow onboard any parts that frequently malfunction, in particular, any unique parts that are difficult to obtain. Refer to the EMERGENCY TOOLS and EMERGENCY REPAIRS sections on the following pages for sample lists of tools and parts you should consider carrying onboard.

In addition, a maintenance/service manual for each piece of equipment that can leave you stranded should be carried as well. Manuals are available from marine publishers such as Technical Publications as well as from some manufacturers.

EMERGENCY REPAIRS

In most cases the problem is minor in nature and can be found and repaired by using good common sense.

The following is a list of some basic spare parts that you should consider carrying onboard your boat; alter the list to fit your needs.

Note that only marine approved parts should be used. **DO NOT** substitute automotive parts.

1. Distributor points
2. Distributor condenser
3. Distributor rotor
4. Distributor cap
5. Coil
6. Coil wire
7. Spark plugs
8. Fuel pump
9. Fuel filter
10. Fuel hose and clamps
11. Propeller
12. Propeller nut and washer
13. Shear pin
14. Cotter key
15. Oil
16. Drain plug
17. Bulb assortment

If you should have problems during an outing, drop your anchor to hold your position. If the water is too deep for a bottom anchor, fabricate a sea anchor by using your bailing bucket or empty fuel can and filling it full of water. Use a rope to tie the sea anchor to the boat's bow.

Diagnose the problem with reference to your troubleshooting manual, then make the adjustment or repair in a systematic manner. Go one step at a time.

If you are unable to get your boat back into operation, refer to pages 78-81 in the *EMERGENCIES* section for rescue procedures.

EMERGENCY TOOLS

A breakdown on water is not a pleasant occurrence. But carrying onboard a few basic hand tools, plus any special tools needed for the boat, motor or drive, will enable you to perform simple repairs that will cure the problem or at least allow you to proceed until a more satisfactory repair can be made. A maintenance/service manual, such as one of those published by Technical Publications, should be onboard.

If your equipment has a history of specific problems, then be prepared to fix those problems as well as other general problems that can occur while boating.

Following is a list of a few basic hand tools that you should consider carrying in your emergency tool box; alter the list to fit your needs.

1. Hammer
2. Pliers (selection)
3. Adjustable wrench
4. Pipe wrench
5. Vise grip
6. Combination wrench set
7. Screwdrivers (selection)
8. Spark plug wrench
9. Spark plug gap gage
10. Test lamp
11. Jumper wire
12. Pocket knife
13. Hand cleaner
14. Towels or rags
15. Tow rope

TOWING VEHICLE

The towing vehicle must be designed or modified to tow the combined weight of boat and trailer. Most average passenger cars are not designed for towing and may perform dangerously if used as such.

As a general rule, the weight of the towing vehicle should equal or exceed the total combined weight of the trailer and its load. The average weight of cars and light trucks has been decreasing and comparing weights of towing vehicle and trailer is very important.

Be sure your car or truck is up to the task of towing the boat and trailer. If you aren't sure, ask your dealer to evaluate your towing vehicle. You might also look up trailer firms in the phone book and ask their recommendations. These firms sometimes modify vehicles so they are better equipped for towing.

If you are buying a new vehicle which will be used for towing, ask the vehicle dealer to explain the manufacturer's towing package option. A towing package increases the towing capability of a vehicle and may include a special engine, limited-slip differential, special rear axle ratio, larger tires and wheels, heavy duty suspension, heavy duty cooling system, automatic transmission cooler, engine oil cooler, oversize alternator and battery, heavy duty brakes and special wiring.

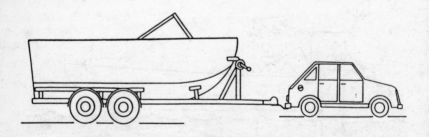

A little car towing a big boat is a bad combination.

HITCH

HITCH CLASSES

Hitches are divided into classes that specify the gross trailer weight (GTW) and maximum tongue weight for each class. Hitch classes are numbered the same and specify the same GTW as the trailer classes.

When selecting a hitch, always use a hitch with the same class number as the trailer, or with a class number that is greater than the trailer. For instance, a class two hitch is mated with a class two trailer. But, a class three or four hitch could also be used with a class two trailer.

HITCH TYPES

There are two basic types of hitches, the weight carrying hitch and the weight distribution (or load equalizer) hitch. Each hitch type is divided into four classes as previously noted.

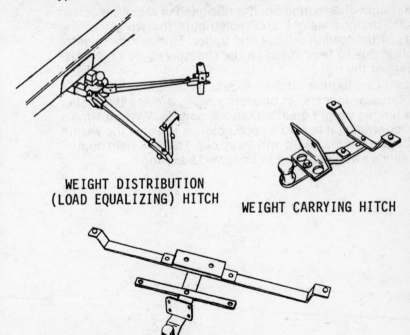

WEIGHT DISTRIBUTION
(LOAD EQUALIZING) HITCH

WEIGHT CARRYING HITCH

WEIGHT CARRYING HITCH

When selecting a hitch towing ball, make sure the ball is of the correct diameter for the intended trailer coupling.

Weight Carrying Hitch

As the name implies, the entire tongue weight of the trailer is carried by the hitch. The hitch is mounted on the rear bumper of the car and is referred to as a "bumper hitch." A bumper hitch is the simplest and cheapest hitch available. Note that the step-bumper hitch used on some trucks is not considered a bumper hitch.

While acceptable for a class one trailer and a class two trailer with a light tongue weight, this type of hitch is unacceptable for the heavier class of trailers.

NOTE: Consult your local state boating agency for hitch recommendations. In some states, weight carrying hitches are considered unsafe and their use is prohibited.

Weight Distribution Hitch

The weight distribution hitch is designed to remove much of the hitch tongue weight and redistribute the weight to the wheels of the towing vehicle and trailer. This results in safer operation due to less strain on the towing vehicle and better handling of the rig.

Weight distribution hitches should be used when towing a class three or four trailer or when towing a class two trailer with a tongue weight greater than 300 pounds. When towing a class four trailer, it is also a good practice to equip the weight distribution hitch with an anti-sway bar. This will help control the trailer's sway resulting in improved handling.

TRAILERS

Be sure your boat is properly loaded and the trailer is securely connected to your towing vehicle before towing your rig to the water. Refer to the following sections for information concerning trailers and related equipment.

You should test drive your rig with it fully loaded. Determine if there are any unsafe handling characteristics that must be corrected. Also assess the pulling and stopping power of the towing vehicle. Practice manuevering the trailer into confined areas. A fully loaded trailer can make a marked difference in the way the towing vehicle handles, so get the feel of your rig now so you don't endanger others on the road later.

Be sure all gear is properly stowed and secured in the boat before towing. NEVER tow your boat with the canvas top or any other canvas covering in the raised position. Be sure you have a spare tire and wheel for the trailer that is in good condition.

If you are unsure about any part of your trailering setup, ask your dealer to inspect your rig.

LEGAL REQUIREMENTS

Like all vehicles on the road, certain legal requirements must be met before you can legally pull your trailer down the road. Contact your state motor vehicle bureau or state police for the legal requirements related to your trailer.

CLASSIFICATIONS

Trailers are separated into four numerical classes based on gross vehicle weight (GVW). Gross vehicle weight is equal to the trailer's weight plus the maximum load it is allowed to carry at a test speed of 60 mph. If the speed is decreased, a slight increase in weight is allowed. However, should the GVW be within 15% of the maximum allowable weight for the class, consideration should be made for selecting the next heavier class of trailer. Trailer classifications are as follows:

CLASS ONE—GVW not over 2000 pounds.

CLASS TWO—GVW over 2000 pounds through 3500 pounds.

CLASS THREE—GVW over 3500 pounds through 5000 pounds.

CLASS FOUR—GVW over 5000 pounds.

IDENTIFICATION PLATE

Federal law requires that each trailer manufacturer fasten an identification plate on the front, left side of each trailer in a location that is clearly visible. The identification plate must display the following: manufacturer, manufacturing date, gross vehicle weight rating (GVWR), front and rear (if applicable) gross axle weight rating (GAWR) with the rated tire size, a statement saying it complies with federal standards, vehicle identification number and vehicle type class.

The combined GAWR of all axles on multi-axle trailers must equal or exceed the trailer's GVWR.

MANUFACTURED BY XXXXX

MFR'D MAY, 1981

GVWR 2945

GAWR FRONT 2995 WITH F78-14 TIRES
REAR N/A WITH N/A TIRES

THIS VEHICLE CONFORMS TO ALL APPLICABLE FEDERAL MOTOR VEHICLE SAFETY STANDARDS IN EFFECT ON THE DATE OF MANUFACTURE SHOWN ABOVE.

YEAR / MODEL 81-T33
VEHICLE I.D. NO.
VEHICLE CLASS: TRAILER

COUPLER AND HITCH BALL

Generally the coupler is one of two basic types, the latch type or the screw type. The coupler is used to attach the trailer to the towing vehicle hitch via the hitch ball.

Coupler and hitch ball size must match for proper mating. Hitch ball size is determined by the trailer class. The minimum ball diameter for a class one trailer is 1 7/8 inches and for class two and three is two inches. If used with a class four trailer the hitch ball and bolt must be of the size and strength to conform with the minimum breaking strength requirements as outlined for that particular gross vehicle weight rating (GVWR).

The coupler rating must not be less than the GVWR of the trailer.

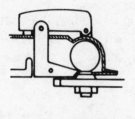

LATCH TYPE

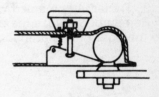

SCREW TYPE

TIE-DOWNS

When a boat is being towed, tie-downs should be used to secure the boat's position on the trailer. If tie-downs are not used, the boat can move unrestrained on the trailer causing possible damage to the hull or the boat can slide off the trailer.

Bow and stern tie-downs are the most important, but other lines should be used if needed. Do not use the winch line as a tie-down; use a separate bow tie-down.

Before tightening any tie-down ropes, be sure the boat rests properly on all trailer supports. Tighten the tie-downs snugly but DO NOT attempt to force the boat against a trailer support by tightening a tie-down as hull damage may result.

SUPPORTS

No boat trailer can duplicate the even pressure of support a boat hull receives from the water. But a boat trailer must support the boat at the best support points on the hull. A boat hull that is improperly supported risks hull damage.

There are two types of supports, rollers and pads. They may be used separately or in combination. As a rule, rollers provide minimum support, but launching and loading are eased because of lower friction. Pads provide maximum support, but launching and loading are harder because of higher friction. Rollers are more desirable if:

1. Trailer is the correct length.
2. Boat hull is properly supported.
3. Supports are correctly positioned.
4. Majority of launching and loading is done from the trailer.
5. Boat is not overloaded or put under any undue stress.

Pads are more desirable if:

1. Boat launching is done by slings or hooks.
2. Trailer is immersed when launching or loading the boat.

Remember, unless the supports are properly used, damage to the boat hull is probable.

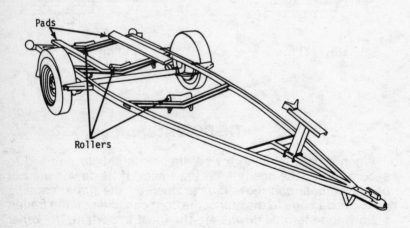

Support Adjustment

Before making any adjustments to the supports, make sure the boat is properly centered on the trailer. The essential sup-

port points on most hulls are:
1. The forefront (just under the bow).
2. The keel line and planking on each side.
3. The turn of the bilge (most important as interior weight is concentrated here).
4. The transom.

Adjust supports to assure equal weight distribution. When one side is adjusted, ensure that the opposite side is properly adjusted to oppose the other. Most rollers and pads can be adjusted up, down, forward and aft to provide the best support. Make adjustments carefully and methodically. Remember, even a minor misalignment can place stress on the whole hull.

Many boat manufacturers claim that most hull damage is incurred by improper trailering of the boat. Ask your dealer to inspect your rig if you think your boat does not fit properly on its trailer.

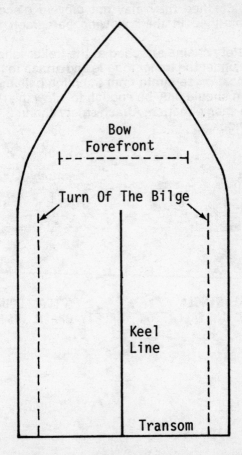

SAFETY CHAINS

Safety chains should be used to prevent disconnection of the trailer and towing vehicle should the hitch ball or trailer coupler fail. Because of differing state requirements, consult your state motor vehicle bureau or state police for the safety chain legal requirements related to your trailer.

If your state does not have a safety chain requirement standard, refer to the following: For class one, two and three trailers, the maximum GVW of each class should be used as the minimum breaking test load of the safety chain and its attachments. For a class four trailer, the gross weight of the trailer including its load should be used as the minimum breaking test load of the safety chain and its attachments.

Even if your rig is equipped with safety chains, if they are not properly attached they may not prevent disconnection. Proceed as outlined in the following paragraph for safety chain usage.

With the safety chains attached at the trailer tongue, cross chain lengths under the trailer tongue and attach to the towing vehicle at a location separate from the hitch ball and bracket. Chain freedom should only be enough to allow the rig to completely turn in each direction. Attach safety chain "S" hooks so they can't unhook.

TYPICAL SINGLE
SAFETY CHAIN INSTALLATION
TYPICAL DOUBLE
SAFETY CHAIN INSTALLATION

BEARING PROTECTORS

Bearing protectors are attached to the wheel hubs in place of the standard dust caps. If your trailer hubs must be submerged when loading or unloading your boat, consider installing bearing protectors.

Bearing protectors hold the grease in the hub under spring-loaded pressure, resulting in a reduced chance of water entering the hub and damaging the bearing assemblies.

If the hubs are immersed in water, it is a good practice to squirt a small amount of grease into the hubs with a hand-operated grease gun. Any water that has found its way into the hubs will be forced out.

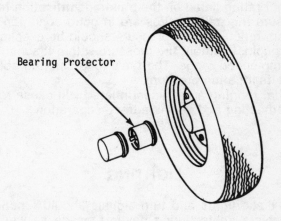

Bearing Protector

TRAILER BRAKES

Because of differing state requirements, contact your state motor vehicle bureau or state police for the trailer brake legal requirements related to your trailer. Most states require trailer brakes on trailers above a certain gross vehicle weight rating (GVWR). Some states also specify which types of brakes are acceptable.

Most popular types of trailer brakes are electric brakes, surge brakes or electrically actuated hydraulic brakes.

Trailer brakes should automatically operate when the brakes of the towing vehicles are applied. In the event of accidental separation of trailer and towing vehicle, the trailer brakes should automatically apply.

Be sure brakes and all associated components are maintained in good working condition. Check operation of brakes at beginning of each season before the first boat outing.

NOTE: Should brakes become submerged in salt water, rinse unit thoroughly with fresh water.

TIRES

Federal law requires that a tire manufacturer display the tire's size, capacity load at maximum pressure and other important information on the tire's sidewall. For each axle, the sum of the tires' capacity load must equal or exceed the gross axle weight rating listed on the trailer identification tag.

Make sure the trailer's tires are in good condition and inspect them regularly. Tire pressure should be checked when the tire is cold. Maintain tire pressure within the manufacturer's recommended range. The tire's load carrying ability will vary with its inflation pressure.

Note that running a tire underinflated will cause rapid tire wear, overheating and possible tread separation.

LIGHTING

Trailer brake lights and turn signals should function with towing vehicle lights during daytime usage as well as tail lights and clearance lights during nighttime usage. Because of the differing state requirements, consult your state motor vehicle bureau or state police for the lighting legal requirements applicable to your trailer.

On vehicles with independent turn signals and stop lights, a converter must be used to adapt the lights to the combination stop/turn signal lights used on the trailer. Stranded automotive wire should be used for trailer wiring as solid core wire is more susceptible to vibration damage.

If trailer must be submerged to launch or load the boat, the service life of the light assemblies will be greatly increased if they are detached so they aren't submerged.

NOTE: Contact between trailer coupler and hitch ball is normally not a good ground and a separate ground wire between trailer and towing vehicle should be used.

LOADING AND BALANCING

An overloaded trailer on the highway can be just as hazardous as an overloaded boat on the water. Know the gross vehicle weight (GVW) of your trailer and do not exceed it. If the GVW is within 15% of the maximum allowable weight for the trailer class, consideration should be made to selecting the next heavier class of trailer.

Trailer tongue weight should be approximately five to seven percent of the GVW. Some towing vehicles will require a lower tongue weight than others. If tongue weight is too light, trailer fishtailing may result as speed increases. If tongue weight is too heavy, excessive strain is put on the towing vehicle and poor handling may result. To check trailer tongue weight proceed as follows:

Weigh the trailer with its normal load to find its GVW. Then, move the tongue of the trailer off the scales. Keep the trailer in a level position and obtain the gross axle weight. Subtract the gross axle weight from the gross vehicle weight (GVW) to find the tongue weight. If tongue weight is not within the proper range, alter the load or its distribution as needed. If correct tongue weight is still not obtained, adjustment of the axle and spring assembly may be required.

Sliding the axle and spring assembly rearward will increase the tongue weight, while sliding the axle and spring assembly forward will decrease the tongue weight.

Remember, safe trailering requires that the trailer is correctly loaded and balanced.

OUTBOARD MOTOR INSTALLATION AND REMOVAL

> **⚠WARNING**
>
> **Be sure outboard motor horsepower does not exceed maximum horsepower rating specified on boat certification plate. Overpowering may produce hazardous operating characteristics.**

Refer to a service manual or ask your dealer if you are unsure as to the correct mounting of your outboard motor. Use only the mounting hardware that is provided by the manufacturer or meets the manufacturer's standards. Note that the use of an inferior grade part may result in early or unexpected failure of a component.

If the outboard motor's weight is beyond your lifting ability, use a suitable hoist and lift bracket or brackets to set the outboard motor on the boat's transom. If a suitable hoist is not available, be sure enough assistance is available to help you handle the outboard motor.

Tighten all the fasteners to the manufacturer's recommendation. Consult your dealer if the manufacturer's recommendations are unknown. Be sure all of the control cables, steering linkage and hydraulic lines are correctly attached and properly adjusted. Check all controls and operation of outboard motor at dock, then recheck tightness of all fasteners and connections. Check maneuvering and operation at slow speed before entering waterway.

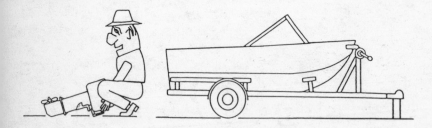

Be sure you can comfortably lift the weight of the outboard motor before attempting installation.

Proper outboard motor transom height is essential to ensure top performance. An outboard motor that is mounted too high on the transom may be affected by ventilation, causing propeller slippage. And an inadequate amount of water will be circulated through the cooling system resulting in overheating of the outboard motor. If the outboard motor is mounted too low on the transom, the excessive drag will result in poor performance.

If you are uncertain about the mounting of the outboard motor on the boat's transom, have your local dealer inspect your rig.

Reverse installation procedure to remove outboard motor from the boat's transom. It is a good practice to make note of all of the settings before the outboard motor is removed. This will ensure the same setting is obtained during installation. DO NOT underestimate the outboard motor's weight, use suitable equipment or be sure enough assistance is available to remove the outboard motor.

BOAT MAINTENANCE

Basic maintenance of your boat can be performed without any mechanical training. Regularly following a maintenance chart that is suited to your needs will help prolong the value and performance of your boat.

You can construct a maintenance chart using the sample on page 139. List items on your chart that need to be inspected and maintained on a scheduled basis. Then ask your dealer to list items that should be periodically inspected in his shop.

If there are items that require inspection or maintenance each time the boat is used, develop a routine you can follow and you'll be less likely to forget.

Half-hearted efforts at maintenance may be more dangerous than no maintenance because you may develop a false feeling of security. To be worthwhile, a maintenance program must be followed so each item is inspected and maintained at its scheduled time.

CONTROLS

⚠WARNING

A malfunctioning boat control mechanism may produce hazardous operating conditions. Proceed directly to shore or do not operate boat if controls do not function properly.

Controls should be checked each time before using boat to ensure proper operation and freedom of movement throughout the full range of operation. Inspect control housing and levers periodically for excessive wear, cracks and other damage. Inspect cables for binding, excessive wear and damage.

Make sure control cable is properly lubricated, adjusted and securely anchored.

Contact your dealer if you are unsure about the operation or servicing of the control system.

STEERING SYSTEM

Periodic inspections of the steering system are a necessity to ensure safe and proper operation.

On a mechanical type steering system, regularly inspect steering components for proper alignment, binding, tension adjustment and damage. In particular, note the condition of the steering cables.

On models with pump-driven power steering or hydraulic steering, inspect all lines and hoses for damage. Check tightness of all fittings and clamps on a regular basis. Maintain correct fluid level.

On models with pump-driven power steering, pulley drive belt should be inspected periodically for tension adjustment, wear and damage. Renew the belt if needed. Maintain proper belt tension to avoid damage to steering components and ensure proper operation.

Contact your dealer for servicing help and recommended lubricants or fluids.

For severe use, including salt water service, more regular inspections are required.

HULL

Aluminum Hulls

Aluminum boats do not usually require extensive care to provide corrosion protection for the hull surface under normal conditions. Exposed aluminum interacts with oxygen in the atmosphere to form a skin covering of aluminum oxide which protects the aluminum underneath. If the hull is painted, contact your dealer for paint recommendations or refer to a maintenance/service manual from a marine publisher such as Technical Publications. The use of improper paint may cause hull surface corrosion.

Aluminum boat hulls must not contact the ground during storage. Acids present in the soil may damage the hull coating and corrode the aluminum. Always store aluminum boats aboveground.

Corrosion may take place at a joint between wood and aluminum if wood has been wet for a long period. Clean, inspect and paint aluminum, then use a suitable bedding compound between the wood and aluminum. The bedding compound forms a separating layer.

On boats constructed with foam flotation material, corrosion can occur at locations where wet foam is in constant contact with aluminum for a long period. Clean and inspect corroded surface, then reinstall foam using foam manufacturer's recommendations. It may be necessary in some instances to apply a moisture barrier type sealant prior to foam installation.

Before the hull is cleaned, you must know what type of aluminum surface is present. The types of unpainted aluminum surfaces that may be encountered are bare aluminum, lacquered, anodized and anodized with a lacquer finish. To test surface for a lacquer coat, apply a drop of lacquer thinner to a lint-free cloth and swab an inconspicuous area. If surface becomes tacky, then lacquer is present. To test surface for anodizing, attempt to clean a small area by rubbing with an eraser. If surface is unblemished when rubbed, then surface is anodized. After surface finish is determined, refer to the following paragraphs for cleaning recommendations.

LACQUERED SURFACE. A lacquered surface is cleaned using water and a mild, non-abrasive detergent. If the lacquer has yellowed, worn-through or weathered thereby requiring renewal of lacquer surface, remove the old lacquer with lacquer thinner then clean the anodized or bare aluminum as outlined in the following paragraphs. Be sure the surface is clean and free of abrasives or residue. Apply a good quality lacquer as recommended by your dealer.

ANODIZED SURFACE. Anodizing is a surface treatment which produces a layer of controlled oxidation that protects the underlying base metal. If the anodized surface cannot be cleaned with mild detergent, a polish of wax with light abrasive content may be used to remove a thin film of unwanted oxidation. Particular care must be used, however, not to rub through the anodized layer. A variety of finishes and thicknesses can be produced through anodizing, so the use of a test area is recommended to obtain best cleaning results.

After cleaning, it may be desirable to apply wax or clear lacquer to reduce cleaning frequency, particularly in a harsh environment.

BARE ALUMINUM SURFACE. Dirt and grease may be removed from a bare aluminum surface by using a non-abrasive cleaner; a solvent may be desirable if grease build-up is excessive.

If the surface cannot be cleaned using a non-abrasive cleaner, then the use of an abrasive polish, such as fine rubbing compound, will be required. Remove as much dirt and grime as possible with soapy water before applying the polish. Rubbing the aluminum with polish will produce a black or dark grey residue which is wiped away with a clean cloth. Reapply the polish and wipe away as necessary to obtain the desired surface finish. Wax or lacquer may be applied after cleaning and polishing to protect the surface.

Liquid brighteners are available which clean and brighten aluminum through chemical action. These brighteners are particularly effective if the surface is heavily oxidized or discolored. Refer to manufacturer's recommendations for method of application. Thoroughly clean treated areas by flushing with water, especially in joints and hidden areas.

Fiberglass Hulls

Fiberglass boat hulls are not maintenance free. The hull surface, known as the gel coat, must be maintained and repaired, when needed, to prevent deterioration of the remaining hull material. Washing the hull will reveal damaged areas and prepare the surface for waxing.

The exterior finish of the hull should be washed periodically using only warm water, mild liquid detergent and a soft-bristled brush or sponge. Do not use an abrasive brush or powders as they could mark the coating surface.

In some cases, oil, grease, stains or scuff marks may be removed by using a cleaning solvent, such as acetone, lacquer thinner or a suitable equivalent. Cleaning solvents should be used very cautiously; extended or excessive application could dissolve the fiberglass. If cleaning solvents are used, be sure to completely rewash the surface before proceeding.

NOTE: Do not allow cleaning solvents to evaporate on the surface. Wipe or pat the surface dry while changing cloths frequently.

Waxing the hull with a good quality marine paste wax will plug the pores and prolong the life and gloss of the hull surface. However, some manufacturers do not recommend waxing their boat's hull. Ask your dealer for advice on waxing your particular boat.

The following precautions should be observed before applying wax:

Use only good quality marine paste wax. Automotive waxes should not be used as they will not fill the pitted pores and may turn white or chalky when exposed to salt water.

Waxes are formulated to be applied either on a damp hull or a completely dry hull. Be sure the correct wax is selected before application.

Do not apply wax on top of anti-fouling paint. The wax coat will form a barrier between the anti-fouling paint and the water thereby defeating the anti-fouling paint's function.

If blistering or other damage is apparent on the hull surface, repair of the damage should be performed as soon as practicable to prevent deterioration of the hull material. Contact your dealer or refer to a maintenance/service manual such as published by Technical Publications for hull repair information. If the hull damage may affect the boat's seaworthiness, ask your dealer to inspect the boat.

HARDWARE

Boat hardware must be inspected and maintained on a regular basis to ensure component luster and prevent corrosion. A more frequent maintenance schedule must be followed if the boat is used in salt water or foul water.

Wash components regularly with soap and water, then thoroughly rinse clean. Use a polish designed for the material (aluminum, chrome plated or stainless steel) you are cleaning. Occasionally apply a protective coating of a suitable wax, then buff clean with a polishing cloth to restore shine.

Keep all hardware fittings tight. Refer to GALVANIC CORROSION later in this section for an explanation of the correct procedure for attaching fittings and fasteners to an aluminum boat.

VINYL SEAT COVERING AND TRIM

Vinyl seat coverings and trim are designed to be water and mildew resistant. Foreign matter can usually be wiped clean with a moist rag or sponge. If necessary, use a mild liquid detergent or a cleanser designed for cleaning vinyl. Some solvents and abrasive detergents may be harmful to vinyl material.

Vinyl material may suffer color fade, dryness and cracking as a result of sun exposure, natural body oils and sun protection lotions. A good practice is to cover vinyl, when not in use, if exposed to sunlight for extended periods. There are vinyl conditioners available which will extend the life of vinyl. Prevent water from entering vinyl seat cover seams to prolong cushion life.

Consult your dealer for any special cleaning or care procedures that apply to your boat.

CARPETING

Most carpeting used on boats is made of all-weather indoor/outdoor synthetic fibers with a rubber backing. Indoor/Outdoor carpet is water repellent, mildew resistant and fade resistant. In most cases, the carpeting can be left wet for a length of time without damage.

To clean carpet, thoroughly scrub with soap and water, then hose down with fresh water. A vacuum may be used to remove dirt and other foreign matter that is embedded in the carpet fibers.

NOTE: If a vacuum cleaner is used on a wet carpet, MAKE SURE that the vacuum cleaner is designed for the intended use.

Consult your dealer or carpeting manufacturer for any special care or cleaning recommendations.

GLASS

Glass used for boat windshields, light covers, hatch covers, windows, etc., is either an approved safety glass or a synthetic glass (plexiglass, clear vinyl, etc.).

Safety glass should either be cleaned with soap and water or by using a good quality cleanser designed for cleaning glass.

Synthetic glass should be washed only with mild soap and water. DO NOT use an abrasive cleanser or cleaning cloth. Use your hand or an approved cleanser to loosen foreign matter. Carefully wipe glass surface dry using a clean, damp chamois.

To ease future cleaning, apply a light protective coating over glass surface using a good quality wax.

NOTE: On synthetic glass, DO NOT use an unapproved glass cleaner or a wax that contains a cleanser. Such use may damage the synthetic glass surface.

CANVAS

Canvas covers must be maintained on a regular basis to ensure usefullness and life expectancy.

Occasionally brushing the canvas with a soft-bristled brush, inside and out, will remove any dust or dirt.

On a regular basis, wash canvas with soap and water, then thoroughly rinse with fresh water. If soiled or mildewed areas are noted, a mixture of ammonia and water or an approved cleaning solution must be used to clean area. Thoroughly wash and rinse out cleaning solution.

To seal a leak in a cover seam, use a paraffin stick and rub along the leaking area or apply a coating of Scotch Guard.

Regular lubrication of snaps and zippers with a suitable lubricant (vaseline, silicone spray, paraffin, etc.) will provide protection and easier operation.

NOTE: At no time fold or roll up a wet canvas. The moisture trapped within may cause mildew.

GALVANIC CORROSION

Galvanic corrosion of aluminum boats is due primarily to the electrolytic action between dissimilar metals, such as aluminum and brass. When the two metals are immersed in a conductive fluid (water), an electric current flows and one metal will be corroded. The corrosion is intensified when the metals contact salt water due to the high conductivity of salt water. Unprotected aluminum is very susceptible to galvanic action and the resultant corrosion.

Galvanic action can be hastened by the presence of stray electric currents. Batteries or any other sources of electricity should be disconnected when not in use.

Aluminum parts are protected by a process known as anodizing which deposits a hard, protective coating of aluminum oxide over the surface. The anodized surface is impervious to corrosion from any source, but is only effective if the anodizing is unbroken. Scratches or abrasions can expose the unprotected metal.

Due to the electrolytic action between dissimilar metals, all fittings and fasteners attached to an aluminum hull should be aluminum or stainless steel. The use of nickel, brass or ferrous fittings and fasterners may result in aluminum corrosion if the fitting or fastener contacts the aluminum. If nickel, brass or ferrous metals must be attached to aluminum, then the surfaces should be insulated with a non-wicking gasket, tape or sealant. Fasteners should be insulated by using nonmetallic sleeves, bushings and washers.

Refer to the previous HULL and HARDWARE sections for care and cleaning procedures of surfaces.

ENGINE AND DRIVE MAINTENANCE

Before operating or servicing any part of the boat's power-train, thoroughly read the manufacturer's operation and maintenance manual. You should also consult with a dealer, even if you didn't buy the boat from a dealer. Ask the dealer if they have any recommendations regarding your boat's engine and drive, and if the manufacturer has made any changes that affect your unit. Now is a good time to inquire about the dealer's service and parts departments in case you will need professional help in the future.

To be effective, a maintenance program must be followed religiously. Skipping scheduled checks will defeat the purpose of maintaining your boat, engine and drive. A good practice is to follow a set pattern of maintenance items that you check every time the boat is used. For less frequent maintenance checks, construct a maintenance chart of items that need to be checked with the recommended interval of time that the checks should be made. A page at the rear of this manual is provided for entering maintenance checks.

The following sections provide some general recommendations. Specific information may be found in the manufacturer's operation and maintenance manual or from manuals published by marine book publishers, such as Technical Publications.

Engine Maintenance

NOTE: In the following *ENGINE MAINTENANCE* section the wording "inboard engine" includes stern drive engines and jet drive engines as well as inboard engines unless stated otherwise.

LUBRICATION

Outboard Motors

All outboard motors are lubricated by oil that is mixed with fuel. The oil is mixed with the fuel either in the fuel tank or at the engine. If the latter system is used, an oil pump pumps oil to the fuel pump, carburetors or intake passages depending on the type of system. The only maintenance required on models with an oil pump is to be sure the oil reservoir contains sufficient oil and all hoses are in good condition.

Inboard Engines

Inboard engines are lubricated by oil contained in an oil pan beneath the engine. Oil is then pumped to the surfaces requiring lubrication.

Consult with your dealer or refer to a maintenance/service manual to obtain the engine manufacturer's recommended oil change interval. Engine oil should be changed more frequently than the manufacturer recommends if the engine undergoes severe usage, such as extensive slow speed operation or short trips, of if the engine is well-worn.

Before attempting to change the oil in an inboard engine, first locate the oil pan drain plug and the oil filter. If either the drain plug or oil filter is inaccessible, you may need professional help. Also determine the oil capacity of the oil pan by asking your dealer or referring to a maintenance/service manual. An oil collector smaller than the oil pan capacity will lead to a messy clean up afterwards. Also be sure the oil collector can be removed without spilling oil after the oil pan is drained.

If an oil collector cannot be used, a small hand-operated oil pump can be used to suck the oil out through the dipstick tube.

Before draining old oil, run engine until it reaches normal operating temperature.

⚠CAUTION

DO NOT operate engine without cooling water being supplied to the raw-water pump on engine or water pump in stern drive. Damage to pump and engine may result without cooling water.

Stop engine and drain old engine oil. Allow oil to drain completely, reinstall drain plug and tighten plug securely.

Remove the oil filter and seal ring; the seal ring usually remains on the filter. Rotate the filter counterclockwise for

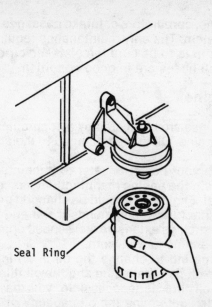

Seal Ring

removal (be prepared to catch oil from filter). In many instances it will be necesary to use a filter removal wrench or
tool to break the filter loose. Discard the old filter and seal
ring. Lightly coat the seal ring on the new filter with oil, then install the new filter. DO NOT overtighten the new filter; it should
be hand-tightened.

Locate the oil fill hole for the engine. On some engines an
oil fill tube is provided while on other engines oil is poured
through a hole in the rocker arm cover. Fill the engine with the
oil type and quantity recommended by the engine manufacturer. DO NOT overfill. Check oil level on oil dipstick. Run
engine for five minutes and check for leaks, particularly
around oil filter. Stop engine, wait five minutes and recheck oil
level on dipstick.

FUEL SYSTEMS

The engine's fuel system, including fuel tanks and lines,
must be maintained to ensure clean fuel is delivered to the
engine and to prevent fire.

The fuel system should be inspected at least once a year at
the beginning of the boating season. It is a good practice to inspect the fuel system at the end of the boating season as well.
If the boat is used year-round, then the system should be inspected at least twice a year.

⚠WARNING

Gasoline is extremely flammable. DO NOT smoke or allow sparks or open flame around fuel or in presence of fuel vapor. Be sure area is well-ventilated. Wipe up spilled fuel immediately. Observe fire prevention rules.

Before starting the engine, inspect the fuel tanks, hoses, clamps and filters. Some systems are also equipped with a fuel/water separator which should be inspected periodically. Filters are often located in the fuel tank, in the fuel line, and on some inboard engines, in the carburetor inlet.

If the condition of a filter element is suspicious, it should be replaced. Filters gradually restrict fuel flow as they accumulate foreign matter. Fuel starvation may not be noticeable until full throttle is required and the engine stumbles, a possibly dangerous situation. Make a note of the condition of the filters as they are replaced and the date. Adjust your inspection timetable accordingly. If the fuel you use is consistently foul, then frequent filter inspections will be required. If filter blockage is a persistent problem, attempt to identify the contaminent then trace the source. Rust particles entering the fuel lines may originate either at your fuel supplier or in your fuel tank. Change fuel suppliers if fuel is the problem.

If the source of rust particles is your fuel tank, correct the problem as soon as possible, before the rust eats through the tank. Ask a mechanic to inspect the tank and determine if the tank can be sealed or repaired, otherwise, the tank must be replaced.

Fuel systems are designed and built to comply with Coast Guard standards. Do not modify the fuel system or install components that are not approved by the Coast Guard. Contact a dealer when in doubt.

If a fuel system component has been serviced, always run engine and check for fuel leaks before using the boat. Remove any spilled fuel IMMEDIATELY.

Fuels which contain alcohol, such as gasohol, can damage fuel systems over an extended period of time. Alcohol can cause deterioration of fuel hoses and lines. Alcohol absorbs water which can cause rust and corrosion in fuel system components. Fuel containing alcohol should only be used if allowed by the engine manufacturer.

ELECTRICAL SYSTEM

The electrical system and components on your boat were designed to comply with Coast Guard standards. Coast Guard approved components are designed to prevent sparks in a compartment containing fuel vapor, such as the engine compartment. Do not modify the electrical system or install components that are not approved by the Coast Guard for marine use. Contact a dealer when in doubt.

Battery

Your boat may be equipped with a battery. There are several different types of marine batteries. If you must replace the battery, install a battery of the same type. Contact your dealer for battery recommendations.

Care must be used when working on or around the battery. Batteries vent explosive hydrogen gas which can be contained in an enclosed engine or battery compartment. Always ventilate the battery or engine compartment before working on or around the battery.

⚠WARNING

Batteries expel explosive hydrogen gas. Be sure battery compartment and area around battery is well-ventilated. DO NOT smoke or allow open flame or sources of spark in area around battery.

⚠WARNING

Batteries contain highly corrosive acid which can spill out if the battery is overturned or the battery case is broken. Protective clothing and eyewear is recommended when handling or servicing batteries. IMMEDIATELY flush with water any area contacting battery fluid then obtain medical aid.

The electrolyte level in the battery should be checked periodically, if possible. Some batteries are constructed so that the electrolyte level cannot be checked. Add distilled water so the electrolyte level reaches the full mark or 3/16 inch above plates. DO NOT overfill. Ask your dealer if you are unsure as to the correct electrolyte level for your battery.

Battery terminals and wire leads must be clean and tight. Protective covers as well as a light coat of grease on the terminals and leads will help prevent corrosion. A neutralizing solution of baking soda and water applied to the terminals and leads will dissolve the corrosion; do not allow solution to enter battery.

Keep the following points in mind:

BE SURE all power is off before disconnecting battery leads from battery terminals.

DO NOT disconnect battery leads from battery terminals when engine is running.

BE SURE to connect negative (grounded) battery lead to negative (−) battery terminal and positive battery lead to positive (+) battery terminal.

Ignition System

Each season the ignition system should be included in a "tune up" to provide efficient engine operation and lessen the possibility of a breakdown. Depending on the complexity of the tune-up procedure, the tune-up may require a professional mechanic or may be performed by someone with the required mechanical expertise. Tune-up specifications are available in marine service and maintenance manuals such as those published by Technical Publications.

Spark plugs can be a particular problem in two-stroke outboard motors, especially if the motor is operated at a speed for which the motor is not designed, for instance, trolling with a motor designed for high speed. The most frequent problem is spark plug fouling due to an accumulation of oil and fuel on the spark plug electrodes. When a two-stroke outboard motor (almost all outboard motors are two-stroke design) begins to miss, the first item to check is the spark plugs (presuming it is not out of gas).

Remove and inspect the spark plugs. If you have any doubt regarding the condition of the plug, install a new spark plug of the type recommended by the engine manufacturer. Refer to a service or maintenance manual for correct spark plug gap.

When installing a spark plug, first be sure the threads and seating surface of the engine are clean. Note if the spark plug is a gasket type plug or uses a tapered seat. Screw the spark plug into the engine until finger-tight, then tighten gasket type plug an additional ¼ turn or tighten the tapered seat plug an additional 1/16 turn. Do not overtighten as the threads in the engine can be damaged.

It is a good practice to keep a set of spark plugs onboard the boat in case the engine's plugs malfunction. A spare spark plug may prevent being stranded.

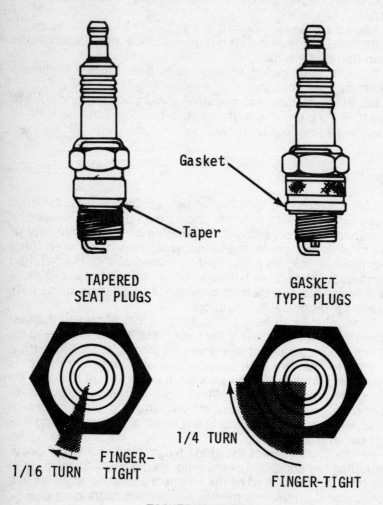

Gasket

Taper

TAPERED
SEAT PLUGS

GASKET
TYPE PLUGS

1/16 TURN   FINGER-
             TIGHT

1/4 TURN

FINGER-TIGHT

TIGHTENING WITH
SOCKET WRENCH

COOLING SYSTEM

Except for air-cooled outboard motors, a water cooling system is used to cool the engine. Water may be pumped from the lower unit to the engine as on outboards and some stern drive units, or a pump mounted on the engine forces water to the engine. Inboard engines may be equipped with open cooling systems (seawater cools the engine directly) or closed cooling systems (seawater passes through a heat exchanger which cools the engine coolant).

Flushing kits are available from your dealer that allow the cooling system to be flushed with clean water. Units used in salt water or water containing silt should be flushed with clean, fresh water as often as possible.

At least twice a year on inboard engines, inspect all cooling system hoses and clamps. Replace any hoses which are cracked, swollen or show other signs of deterioration.

Inboard engines with a closed cooling system should be drained, flushed and refilled with an antifreeze or rust inhibitor solution at least once each year. Consult your dealer for proper procedure and cooling system capacity.

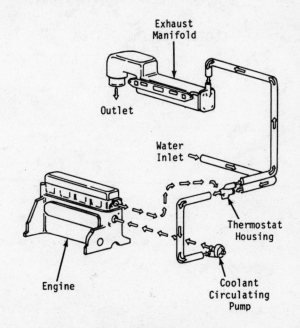

OPEN COOLING SYSTEM

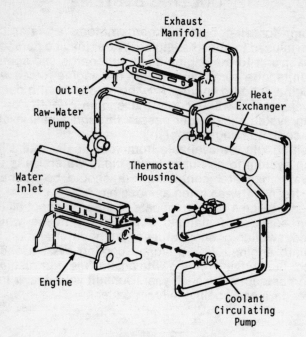

Exhaust
Manifold

Outlet

Raw-Water
Pump

Water
Inlet

Heat
Exchanger

Thermostat
Housing

Engine

Coolant
Circulating
Pump

CLOSED COOLING SYSTEM

DRIVE BELTS

Most inboard engines are equipped with equipment such as an alternator and water pump which are driven by a V-belt connected to the crankshaft pulley.

Periodically inspect the condition of the drive belts for signs of wear and deterioration. If the belt is cracked, frayed or excessively worn then it should be replaced.

To remove the belt and install a new belt, belt tension must be released so the belt can be moved off the pulley. Loosen the screw in the adjustment slot of the bracket securing the alternator or pump and slightly loosen any remaining fasteners. Push the alternator or pump towards the engine. There should be sufficient slack now to remove the belt. In some cases it will be necessary to remove other belts before removing the belt you want.

Install the same size belt as the removed belt, presuming the old belt was the right size. To adjust belt tension, pull the alternator or pump away from the engine so there is approximately ½-inch deflection when light thumb pressure is applied against the belt at the midpoint between the pulleys. If the belt contacts more than two pulleys, check belt tension between the farthest pulleys. Tighten all fasteners.

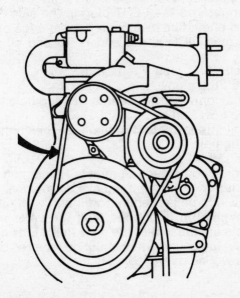

GALVANIC CORROSION

Refer to *DRIVE MAINTENANCE* section for a description of galvanic corrosion.

Some inboard engines are equipped with anodes to prevent galvanic corrosion of engine components. The anodes should be inspected periodically. The frequency of inspection is determined by the rate the anodes are consumed. Install a new anode when the existing anode has been consumed to less than half its original size.

Drive Maintenance

LUBRICATION

Outboard Motors

The gears, shafts and bearings in the lower unit of an outboard motor are lubricated by oil contained in the housing.

Most manufacturers recommend checking the lubricant level in the lower unit after 30 to 50 hours of operation. The lubricant should be drained after 100 hours of operation or after each season, whichever occurs first, then new lubricant should be installed.

To check oil level in lower unit, place outboard in a vertical position then remove the VENT plug in the side of the lower unit. Oil level should be even with bottom edge of hole. If oil level is low then oil must be added. To add oil proceed as follows:

1. Reinstall VENT plug if removed.
2. Remove FILL plug.
3. Insert oil container nozzle into fill plug hole.
4. Remove VENT plug.
5. Force oil into lower unit until oil reaches bottom edge of vent plug hole.
6. Reinstall VENT plug.
7. Remove oil container and reinstall FILL plug.

To drain oil from lower unit remove both plugs. After draining oil, follow add oil procedure to fill unit with oil.

NOTE: Anytime oil is drained look for water in the oil. If water droplets are present or the oil is milky brown, then there is a leak in the lower unit which must be repaired or lower unit components will be damaged.

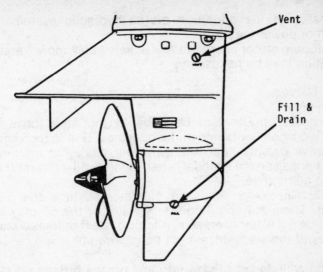

Vent

Fill &
Drain

Some outboards are equipped with three plugs, VENT, FILL and DRAIN. The fill plug is adjacent to the vent plug. To fill or add lubricant on these units, the drain plug must be installed and the vent and fill plugs must be removed. Force lubricant into the gear housing through the fill opening until oil reaches the bottom of the vent plug hole. Reinstall the vent and fill plugs.

On some smaller outboard motors there is only one hole; there is no vent hole. Add oil by laying the outboard on its side then fill with oil until full.

Periodically inject grease into any grease fittings on outboard motor and lubricate linkage. At least once each season remove propeller and lubricate propeller shaft and threads with water resistant grease.

⚠WARNING

Be sure ignition is "OFF" and gear selector is in "NEUTRAL" when servicing propeller, otherwise, accidental starting can occur if propeller shaft is rotated.

Inspect hydraulic hoses, fittings and cylinders for signs of leakage. Inspect hydraulic hoses for cracking and other signs of deterioration. Hoses must not rub against objects which can damage hose. Professional help should be sought if you are unsure of the condition of the hydraulic systems for tilt/trim or power steering.

If outboard motor is used in foul or salt water, more frequent lubrication may be necessary.

Stern Drives

The gears, shafts and bearings in the stern drive are lubricated by oil contained in the housings. Due to the various stern drive designs, consult with your dealer or refer to a maintenance/service manual when adding oil or completely refilling stern drive.

NOTE: Check for presence of water anytime the oil is drained. There may be droplets of water or the oil may turn milky brown if water is present. A leak exists if there is water in the oil and the stern drive must be repaired or it will be damaged.

Periodically inject grease into any grease fittings on stern drive and components between engine and stern drive. It is necessary to remove the stern drive to reach all lubrication points on some models; consult with your dealer or refer to a maintenance/service manual.

Inspect hydraulic hoses, fittings and cylinders for signs of leakage. Inspect hydraulic hoses for cracking and other signs of deterioration. Hoses must not rub against objects which can damage hose. Professional help should be sought if you are unsure of the condition of the hydraulic systems for tilt/trim or power steering.

Inspect rubber boots, bellows and clamps on stern drive units so equipped. Replace any damaged or worn boot, bellows or protective cover.

At least once each season, remove the propeller and lubricate the propeller shaft and threads with water-resistant grease.

⚠WARNING

Be sure ignition is "OFF" and gear selector is in "NEUTRAL" when servicing propeller, otherwise, accidental starting can occur if propeller shaft is rotated.

If boat is operated in foul or salt water, more frequent maintenance intervals may be necessary.

Inboard Drives And Jet Drives

Lubrication requirements for jet drives and inboard transmissions, V-drives and drive components vary according to manufacturer, usage and boat design. Consult with your dealer or refer to a maintenance/service manual for lubrication recommendations.

GALVANIC CORROSION

The aluminum-silicon alloys used for motor and drive unit castings are relatively resistant to corrosion from oxidation, but are very susceptible to galvanic action and the resultant corrosion if unprotected.

Galvanic action is an electrical process where atoms of one metal are carried in a solution (water) and deposited on the surface of a dissimilar metal. Chrome or nickel plating are controlled forms of galvanic action. Each metallic element has a particular degree of susceptibility to galvanic corrosion, and pure aluminum is second only to magnesium in this scale. The aluminum alloys are somewhat less susceptible than pure metal, and galvanic action can be effectively stopped by painting or other surface protection.

Galvanic corrosion can be a real problem.

Galvanic corrosion is more active in salt water because of the presence of minerals in the water which makes it more effective as a conductor. Operation in salt water requires some special care to combat the possibility of corrosion. The drive unit should be raised out of the water after each use and the outside surface rinsed with fresh water immediately after each use. On models that circulate salt water throughout components as a coolant, fresh water should be used to flush system after each use.

Protection against galvanic corrosion is generally accomplished by attaching a small block of more susceptible metal in the water near the part to be protected. This block of metal is known as the anode. Anodes are attached directly to the drive unit in most cases and are usually shaped as a removable plate or plug. On some drive units the trim tab is the anode. Anodes should be replaced if more than half the original size is corroded away. Be sure the new anode makes good contact with the mounting surface; scrape mounting surface if necessary.

All motor and drive unit castings, especially those used in salt water, should have an adequate coverage of paint. Use only an approved paint applied according to manufacturer's instructions. DO NOT paint anodes.

NOTE: Most manufacturers do not recommend the use of anti-fouling paint on motor or drive unit castings. Anti-fouling paints contain mercury or copper which can cause galvanic corrosion in the presence of aluminum.

WINTERIZING

Discussed in the following sections are accepted practices for storing your boat, motor and drive through the winter. Some manufacturers recommend specific procedures which they feel should be followed to properly store or winterize their products. Consult your dealer for the manufacturer's recommendations.

NOTE: Fuel containing alcohol should be drained or emptied during storage. Alcohol blended fuels will cause faster deterioration of elastomers, e.g., hoses and gaskets. If phase separation occurs during storage, the alcohol will sink to the bottom of the tank and corrosion will result.

MOTOR

Outboard Motor

The following list of procedures should be adapted to fit your needs.

With the outboard motor still mounted on the boat and operating in fresh water:

1. Run the engine until normal operating temperature is reached.
2. With the gear shift placed in the neutral position and the engine running at part throttle, rapidly inject a rust preventative oil into the carburetor air intake, or intakes, (10-20 seconds) until the engine begins to smoke abundantly or dies.

Remove the boat and motor from the water, then:

3. Drain the fuel from the carburetor, fuel lines, filters and tanks. If any fuel spillage occurs, wipe it up immediately. Store fuel tanks and fuel lines in a well-ventilated area.
4. Completely close the throttle lever. Disconnect the spark plug leads and properly ground them.
5. Turn the engine over several times with the electric or manual starter to expel all water from the cooling system.
6. Clean and lubricate all of the linkage with a lubricant recommended by the manufacturer.
7. Remove the propeller. Inspect the propeller shaft seals for leakage and renew if needed. Apply a thin coating of the manufacturer's recommended lubricant on the propeller shaft.

8. Drain and refill the lower gear housing with a lubricant recommended by the manufacturer.
9. Apply a light film of oil over the exterior of the engine or spray with an anti-corrosion compound.
10. Apply a protective coating of wax to the engine cover using a good quality marine type wax.
11. Store the outboard motor in an upright position in an area that is dry and well-ventilated. If a cover is used over the engine cover, make sure air is allowed to circulate freely to ensure evaporation of any condensation.
12. Remove the battery from the boat. Charge the battery to full charge, then store in a cool, well-ventilated area. Periodically check the battery's condition and recharge, if necessary, using a trickle charger.

Stern Drive, Inboard or Jet Drive Engine

The following list of procedures should be adapted to fit your needs.
With the boat still in the water:
1. Start the engine and allow it to run until normal operating temperature is reached. Stop the engine and allow it to cool for approximately ten minutes, then change the engine oil and filter. Use the oil and filter recommended by the manufacturer. Start the engine and allow it to run to circulate the oil, then stop the engine and allow the oil to drain down. Check the oil level and, if necessary, add oil to obtain the correct level.
2. Remove the flame arrester. Start the engine and run at fast idle. Slowly pour a rust preventative oil into the carburetor air intakes. If the engine does not die, turn it off immediately.

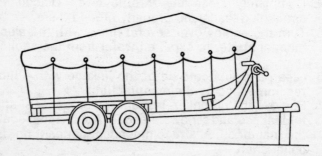

Remove the boat from the water, then:

3. If a closed cooling system is used, check the anti-freeze for contamination and its freezing point. Be sure the freezing point is below the lowest temperature it will be exposed to. If the anti-freeze is more than one season old, a rust inhibitor should be added. If the anti-freeze solution is contaminated, flush and renew solution with a 50/50 mixture of ethylene glycol anti-freeze and water.

4. If a raw-water cooling system is used, open all engine and manifold water jacket drains (consult your dealer if uncertain of the drain locations) and allow all water to drain out. Probe the holes with a length of wire to keep all drain openings clear. Note that if the engine was used in salt water, the cooling system must be flushed out with fresh water. Leave all of the drains open. Disconnect all lower water hoses and allow them to drain. If a water pocket will not drain, add anti-freeze to the water or use a small pump and draw the water out. Drain the water pump, or pumps, and remove the pump impeller, or impellers, if so instructed by the manufacturer.

5. Renew all of the fuel filters.

6. If a non-alcohol blend of fuel is used, top off the fuel tank and add the appropriate amount of fuel stabilizer. If an alcohol blend of fuel is used, the complete fuel system should be drained.

7. Clean and lubricate all of the linkage with a lubricant recommended by the manufacturer.

8. Seal the carburetor and exhaust manifold openings to prevent foreign matter from entering.

9. Remove the battery from the boat. Charge the battery to full charge, then store in a cool, well-ventilated area. Periodically check the battery's condition and recharge, if necessary, using a trickle charger.

DRIVES

Outboard Drive And Stern Drive

1. Drain and refill the gearcases with a lubricant recommended by the manufacturer.

2. Clean and lubricate all of the linkage with a lubricant recommended by the manufacturer.

3. Apply a light film of oil over the exterior of the drive unit or spray with an anti-corrosion compound.

4. Store the drive unit in the down position.

Inboard Drive

1. Drain and refill the transmission with a lubricant recommended by the manufacturer.
2. Inspect the propeller shaft and rudder post stuffing boxes. If damage is noted, consult your dealer for repair or renewal of the stuffing boxes.
3. Clean and lubricate all of the linkage with a lubricant recommended by the manufacturer.
4. Inspect all other components and repair or renew if needed.

BOATS

Fiberglass Boats

After removing the boat from the water, completely inspect the hull for any type of damage. If damage is noted, arrangements should be made for hull restoration during the off-season.

Completely wash and clean the outside of the hull as outlined on page 105. As a good practice, the interior and top surfaces should be cleaned for best preservation and to lower the work load next spring.

Store the boat on a trailer with the bow placed higher than the stern. Remove all of the inner hull drain plugs and the transom drain plug. If a boat cover is used, make sure air is allowed to circulate freely to ensure evaporation of any condensation.

If the boat is not stored on a trailer, the manufacturer's recommendations for supporting the boat must be followed.

Aluminum Boats

After removing the boat from the water, completely inspect the hull for any type of damage. If damage is noted, arrangements should be made for hull restoration during the off-season.

Wash and clean the outside of the hull as outlined on page 104. As a good practice, the interior and top surfaces should be cleaned for best preservation and to lower the work load next spring. Completely drain all water.

Larger boats should be stored with the bow higher than the stern and the transom drain plug removed. Smaller boats should be stored upside down with the bow slightly higher than the stern. If a boat cover is used, make sure air is allowed to circulate freely to assure evaporation of any condensation.

Aluminum boats should never be stored directly on the ground. Ground acids, especially during the spring and fall months, are very corrosive to aluminum. If the boat is not stored on a trailer, the manufacturer's recommendations for supporting the boat must be followed.

RETURNING TO SERVICE

The following list of procedures should be adapted to fit your needs when returning equipment to service after seasonal storage.

All Engines

1. Check engine alignment and make sure all engine fasteners are tight.
2. Install all drain plugs and close drain valves.
3. Note all of the fluid levels and correct if needed.
4. Renew all of the spark plugs.
5. Check all of the electrical wiring for looseness or damage and tighten or renew if needed.
6. Readjust the drive belt's tension if needed. Renew the drive belt if damage is noted.
7. Renew any hoses or hose clamps if needed.
8. If the gasoline was stored, drain and renew if gummy deposits are noted.
9. Make sure the battery is fully charged, then reinstall. Clean the positive and negative battery posts and cable ends. Match the cable ends to the battery posts, then secure and lightly grease to prevent corrosion.
10. Have all of the engine settings checked by your dealer.

All Drive Units

1. Note all the components for any type of damage and renew if needed.
2. Check all of the components for looseness and tighten if needed.
3. Check all of the gearcases for the correct amount of lubricant.
4. Make sure all control linkage and steering linkage operates freely and correctly.

ORGANIZATIONS

American Boat and Yacht Council (ABYC)
P.O. Box 806
Amityville, NY 11701

American National Red Cross
17th & D Streets, N.W.
Washington, D.C. 20006

American Water Ski Association (AWSA)
S.R. 542 & Carl Floyd Road
Winter Haven, FL 33880

Boat/U.S. Foundation
880 South Pickett Street
Alexandria, VA 22304

National Marine Manufacturers Association (NMMA)
401 North Michigan Avenue
Chicago, IL 60611

National Ocean Service
Distribution Branch
Riverdale, MD 20737

Technical Publications Division
Intertec Publishing Corp.
P.O. Box 12901
Overland Park, KS 66212

United States Coast Guard
2100 Second St., S.W.
Washington, D.C. 20593

United States Power Squadrons
P.O. Box 30423
Raleigh, NC 27617

U.S. Army Corps of Engineers
Department of the Army
20 Massachusetts Avenue, N.W.
Washington, D.C. 20314

GLOSSARY

The following list of terms are commonly used boating terms and are provided here as a handy reference. Other boating and nautical terms will be found in a comprehensive dictionary.

Abaft — behind; toward the rear
Abeam — a line at right angles to a boat's keel
Adrift — untied; floating without direction or anchoring
Aft — toward the rear or stern of the boat
Amidships — center or middle of the boat
Astern — behind a boat
Ballast — a heavy article added to provide greater stability
Beam — a boat's widest width
Bearing — relative position or direction
Bilge — lowest interior part of the boat hull
Binnacle — the housing containing the boat's compass
Bow — the front part of a boat
Broach — to dangerously turn a boat parallel to the waves, permitting possible capsizing
Bulkhead — an upright wall in a boat
Bulwark — the side of the boat that is above the deck
Chine — the point on a boat where the side meets the bottom
Chock — a fitting used as a line guide
Cleat — a mounted deck fitting with ears on which lines are fastened
Draft — the depth of water that a boat displaces
Drive Unit — includes gears and shafts contained in a housing, such as the lower portion of an outboard motor or the housing and gear assembly of a stern drive
Fathom — a unit of depth or length, one fathom equals six feet
Fender — a guard used for cushioning, e.g., boat to dock
Fore — toward the front or bow of the boat
Foul — tangled
Freeboard — vertical length from deck to waterline
Gunwale — the point on a boat where the hull and deck meet
Head — boat toilet compartment
Heel — to lean to a side
Helm — the wheel by which a boat is steered
Keel — backbone of a boat; extends along the length of the boat's bottom
Knot — one nautical mile an hour (one nautical mile equals approximately 6,076 feet); a unit for measuring boat speed; knots x 1.15 = mph

Lee — the side of the boat that is sheltered from the wind

Leeward — direction which is away from the wind

Leeway — an off-course lateral movement due to wind or current

List — the tilt or lean to one side of a boat

Lower Unit — the lower housing of an outboard motor or stern drive that contains the propeller shaft, drive gears and lower drive shaft end

Mooring — a location where a boat is held or secured in place using lines, cables or anchor

Planing — rising partly out of the water when underway

Port — the left side of a boat when looking forward

Rudder — a flat piece hinged vertically at the stern of the boat used for steering

Scupper — overboard drain holes on deck

Sea Anchor — any device thrown overboard to reduce a boat's drift and to keep it headed into the wind

Skeg — extension of keel for protection of propeller and rudder

Stanchion — an upright support post

Starboard — the right side of a boat when looking forward

Stern — the aft end of a boat

Strake — a line of planking extending from bow to stern along the sides and bottom of a boat; strakes may be formed into a hull during construction

Stringer — fore and aft strip on inner side of hull for additional structural strength

Transom — a transverse beam across the stern of the boat

Trim — fore and aft balance of the boat

Wake — the track or path left in the water by a moving boat

Windward — direction which is toward the wind

Yaw — unintentional deviation or turning off course, possibly due to rough water

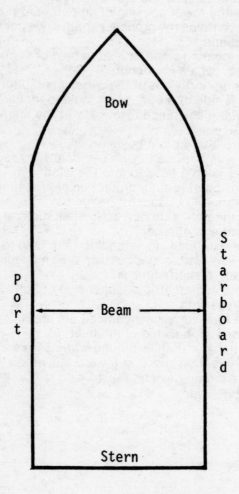

Diagram showing relationship of port and starboard sides of boat when viewed from above.

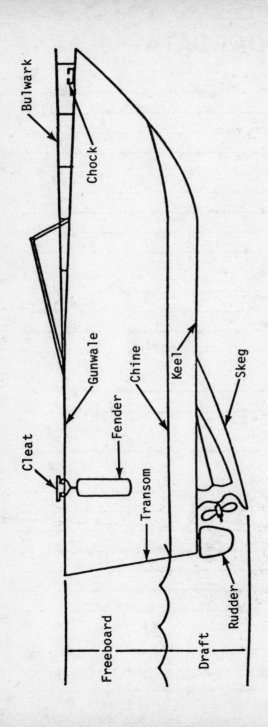

Drawing depicting some descriptive boat terms.

BOAT DATA

OWNER
Name _____
Address _____
_____
Home Phone _____

DEALER
Name _____
Address _____
_____
Business Phone _____

BOAT
Make/Model _____
Serial No. _____
State Registration No. _____
Date of Purchase _____ Key No. _____

ENGINE
Make/Model _____
Serial No. _____

DRIVE UNIT
Serial No. _____

INSURANCE
Company _____
Policy No. _____
Agent _____
Address _____
_____
Business Phone _____
Home Phone _____

OTHER
_____
_____
_____

TRAILER DATA

OWNER

Name _____

Address _____

_____

Home Phone _____

DEALER

Name _____

Address _____

_____

Business Phone _____

TRAILER

Make/Model _____

Serial No. _____

LICENSE NUMBER

Towing Vehicle _____

Trailer _____

INSURANCE

Company _____

Policy No. _____

Agent _____

Address _____

_____

Business Phone _____

Home Phone _____

OTHER

_____

IMPORTANT MAINTENANCE INFORMATION

Recommended Fluids —

_____

_____

_____

_____

_____

Part Numbers —

_____

_____

_____

_____

_____

Marina or Parts Store Telephone Numbers —

_____

_____

_____

_____

MAINTENANCE CHART

Service Interval

Maintenance Job

MAINTENANCE CHART

Service Interval

Maintenance Job

OWNER'S LOG

Date	Log Entry

OWNER'S LOG

Date	Log Entry

MANUFACTURER'S ADDRESSES

Boat, motor and drive manufacturer's addresses are listed on the following pages. Note that this is only a partial listing of manufacturers.

BOAT MANUFACTURERS

ADVANTAGE
See Baretta

AEROCRAFT
Aerocraft Boats
339 Bidwell Rd.
Coldwater, MI 49036

AERO-GLASS
Aero-Glass Boat Co.
310 Bridgeway Ave.
Old Hickory, TN 37138
615-846-5258

AGGRESSOR
Aggressor Boats
P.O. Box 507
Willachoochee, GA 31650
912-534-5270

ALBIN
Albin Marine, Inc.
143 River Road
Cos Cob, CT 06807
203-661-4341

ALLISON CRAFT
Louisville Marine Distributors
Route 4, Box 1-A
Louisville, TN 37777
615-983-5920

ALOHA
Wa-Co Mfg., Inc.
3700 Crutcher St.
No. Little Rock, AR 72118

ALUMA CRAFT
Aluma Craft Boat Co.
315 West St. Julien St.
St. Peter, MN 56082
507-931-1050

AMERICAN FIBER-LITE
American Fiber-Lite
P.O. Box 67
Marion, IL 62959
618-997-5474

AMERICAN SKIER
American Skier Boat Corp.
301 Enterprise Dr.
Ocoee, FL 32761
305-656-3332

ANACAPRI
Anacapri Marine Inc.
3660 N.W. 41st Street
Miami, FL 33142
305-635-7502

ANGLER
Angler Boat Corp.
4450 N.W. 128th St.
Miami, FL 33054
305-681-4990

ANKOR CRAFT
Scott Boat Co. Inc.
801 Fourth Street
Tell City, IN 47586
812-836-2480

ANSWER MARINE
Answer Marine Inc.
9500 N.W. 36 Ave.
Miami, FL 33147
305-836-1033

APPLE LINE
Apple Line Co.
146 Church St.
Amsterdam, NY 12010

AQUA CRUISER
Aqua Cruiser Inc.
Box 1055
Columbia, TN 38401
615-388-4800

AQUASPORT
Aquasport, Inc.
7925 West 2nd Ct.
Hialeah, FL 33014
305-822-1921

ARISTO CRAFT
Aristocraft Boat Corp.
P.O. Box 8238
Atlanta, GA 30306
404-874-0893

ARROW GLASS
See Eldocraft

ARTCRAFT
Scott Fiberglass Products
579 Buddy Williamson Rd.
New Market, AL 35761
205-828-3153

ASTROGLASS
Astroglass Boat Co.
P.O. Box 720
Murfreesboro, TN 37130
615-890-1593

AVANTI
Avanti Ind., Inc.
9434 Dovetail Dr.
Cordova, TN 38018
901-755-4974

AVENGER
Cee Bee Mfg. Co.
11511 Bellinger St.
Lynwood, CA 90262

BAHA
Baha Cruisers Inc.
P.O. Box 659
Perry, FL 32347
904-584-2161

BAJA
Baja Boats
P.O. Box 1009
Bucyrus, OH 44820
419-562-5377

BARETTA
Mel-Hart Products Inc.
1052 Harrison Street
Conway, AR 72032
800-643-8369

BASS CAT
Bass Cat Boats
P.O. Box 511
Mountain Home, AR 72653
501-481-5135

BASSMASTER
Bassmaster Boats
Box 803
Danville, KY 40422
606-236-5601

BASSTRACKER
Pro Bass Shops
P.O. Box 4046
Springfield, MO 65808
417-887-1915

BAYLINER
Bayliner Marine Corp.
P.O. Box 24467
Seattle, WA 98134
206-435-5571

MANUFACTURER'S ADDRESSES (BOAT)

BEACHCOMBER
Boats Unlimited Corp.
1520 Peavy
Dallas, TX 75218

BEACHCRAFT
Beachcraft Marine Corp.
P.O. Box 12455
Salem, OR 97309
503-363-3511

BELL BOY
American Marine Industries
2556 E. 11th Street
Tacoma, WA 98421

BERTRAM
Bertram Yacht
3663 N.W. 21st St.
Miami, FL 33142
305-633-8011

BLACK FIN
Black Fin Yacht Corp.
P.O. Box 22982
Ft. Lauderdale, FL 33335
305-525-6314

BLACK RIVER
Black River Canoes, Inc.
167 Railroad St.
Box 537
La Grange, OH 44050
216-355-4293

BLUE FIN
Blue Fin Industries
P.O. Box 130
New Paris, IN 46553
219-831-4250

BLUE HOLE
The Blue Hole Canoe Co.
Sunbright, TN 37872

BLUE WATER
Blue Water Boats
307 Q Street
Springfield, OR 97477
503-741-1111

BLUEWATER YACHTS
Bluewater Yachts
811 E. Maple
Mora, MN 55051
612-679-3811

BOAT-CRAFT
Tech Boats Inc.
9221 Quivira Rd.
Overland Park, KS 66215

BOATEL
Boatel Catamarans Inc.
811 East Maple
Mora, MN 55051

BOMBER
Fiberking, Inc.
P.O. Box 376
Smyrna, TN 37167
615-244-1537

BONANZA
Bonanza Molding Corp.
Rt. 3, Hwy. 54 So.
Box 80
Eldon, MO 65026
314-392-3131

BONICRAFT
Fibercraft Inc.
P.O. Box 308
Winona Lake, IN 46580
219-267-2567

BONITO
Bonito Boats Inc.
P.O. Box 5728
Orlando, FL 32805

BORUM
Borum Boats Inc.
1900 Wambolt Street
Jacksonville, FL 32202

BOSTON WHALER
Boston Whaler, Inc.
1149P Hingham St.
Rockland, MA 02370
617-871-1400

BROWNING AEROCRAFT
Browning Aero Craft Marine
P.O. Box 501
Decatur, IN 46733

BRUNO & STILLMAN
Bruno & Stillman
23 Old Dover Road
Newington, NH 03801
603-431-8055

BUCCANEER
Buccaneer Power Boats
P.O. Box 63
Cord, AR 72524

BURNS CRAFT
Burns Mfg., Inc.
2940 East Avalon
Muscle Shoals, AL 35661

C-CRAFT
Wenzel Fiberglass Boat Co., Inc.
Rt. 1, Deep Creek Lake
McHenry, MD 21541

CADDO
Caddo Boat Mfg. Co. Inc.
4071 Shilling Way
Dallas, TX 75237
214-339-9422

CAJUN
Mastercrafters Corp.
Rte. 3, Box 333
Winnsboro, LA 71295
318-435-3171

CAMPION
Campion, Inc.
3601 N.W. Yeon
Portland, OR 97210

CANE CUTTER
Cane Cutter, Inc.
300 Washington St.
Bastrop, LA 71220

CARAVELLE
Fiberglass-Plastics, Inc.
P.O. Box 753
Jacksonville, AR 72076
501-982-0504

CARGILE
Cargile Inc.
999 Polk Avenue
Nashville, TN 37211
615-244-1397

CARIBE
Nuco Boats, Inc.
Road 1, Box 200
Greensburg, PA 15601
412-351-2747

CARLCRAFT
Laminated Products Inc.
212 E. Cedar St.
Goodlettsville, TN 37072

CARVER
Carver Boat Corp.
331 1st Street, Box L
Pulaski, WI 54162
414-822-3214

CARY
C. K. Industries Inc.
3391 S.E. 14th Ave.
Port Everglades, FL 33316

CELEBRITY
Celebrity Boats, Inc.
P.O. Box 394
Benton, IL 62812
618-439-9444

CENTURION
Fineline Ind., Inc.
455 Grogan Ave.
Merced, CA 95340
209-384-0255

CENTURY
Century Boat Co.
P.O. Box 519
Manistee, MI 49660
616-723-9975

CHALLENGER (AL)
Tennessee Valley Fbg., Co., Inc.
3310 N. Hilo Circle, N.E.
Huntsville, AL 35810
205-837-8342

MANUFACTURER'S ADDRESSES (BOAT)

CHAMPION
Champion Boat Co.
P.O. Box 652
Mountain Home, AR 72653
501-425-5626

CHAPARRAL
Chaparral Boats, Inc.
P.O. Drawer 928
Nashville, GA 31639
912-686-7484

CHARGER
Charger, Inc.
P.O. Box 709
Richland, MO 65556
314-765-3267

CHEATER-SX
Astroglass Boat Co.
P.O. Box 205
Pleasant View, TN 37146

CHECKMATE
Checkmate Boats
P.O. Box 723
Bucyrus, OH 44820
419-562-5027

CHEETAH
Cheetah Boats
P.O. Box 205
Pleasant View, TN 37146
615-746-5845

CHEROKEE
McKenzie Boat Mfg. Co.
121 No. Highland Dr.
McKenzie, TN 38201

CHESTNUT
Chestnut Canoe Co., Ltd.
Oromocto, NB, Canada
E2V 2G5

CHRIS CRAFT
Murray Industries
Box 860
Pompano Beach, FL 33060
305-946-4000

CHRYSLER
Texas Marine International Inc.
P.O. Box 218
Plano, TX 75074

CIMMARON
See EBKO

CITATION (IN)
All Season Industries Inc.
P.O. Box 327
Markle, IN 46770

CITATION (SC)
Fiberskiff, Inc.
P.O. Box 219
Chapin, SC 29036
803-345-3282

CLASSIC
Classic Boats, Inc.
1 So. Roselle Rd.
Roselle, IL 60172

CLINTON
Riehl Mfg. Co.
2032 State Road
Port Clinton, OH 43452
419-732-2223

COBALT
Cobalt Boats
Twin Rivers Industrial Park
Neodesha, KS 66757
316-325-2653

COBIA
Cobia Boat Co.
P.O. Box 1857
Sanford, FL 32771
305-322-3540

COBRA
Cobra Boat Co.
1012 Meridian Street
Huntsville, AL 35811

COLEMAN
The Coleman Co. Inc.
P.O. Box 1762
Wichita, KS 67201
316-261-3476

COLLINS CRAFT
Collins Craft, Inc.
230 Chumuckla Hwy.
Pace, FL 32570

CONCORD
Concord Boat Corp.
7901 Warden Road
Sherwood, AR 72116
501-834-1759

CONROY
Conroy Industries
3355 Cherry Ridge Dr.
San Antonio, TX 78230

CONTINENTAL
Continental Boats Inc.
257-259 W. 23rd Street
Hialeah, FL 33010

COOCHEE CRAFT
Coochee Craft Boat Co.
P.O. Box 507
Willachoochee, GA 31650
912-534-5270

CORE CRAFT
Bemidji Boat Co. Inc.
Box 249, Hwy. 2 West
Bemidji, MN 56601
218-751-2254

CORRECT CRAFT
Correct Craft, Inc.
P.O. Box 13389
Orlando, FL 32859
305-855-4141

CREST
Maurell Products, Inc.
2711 South M-52
Owosso, MI 48867

CRESTLINER
Nordic Boat Co., Inc.
1501 Crestview Dr.
Little Falls, MN 56345
612-632-6686

CRITCHFIELD
Sabre Marine, Inc.
11300 Space Blvd.
Orlando, FL 32809
305-857-1680

CRUISE CAT
G Group, Inc.
50051 Scheenhen Road
Utica, MI 48087

CRUISERS
Cruisers, Inc.
804 Pecor St.
Oconto, WI 54153
414-834-2211

CUSTOM CRAFT
Custom Fiberglass
   Manufacturers, Inc.
P.O. Box 572
Metter, GA 30439
912-685-5040

DARGEL
Dargel Boat Works
Rt. 1, Box 124
Donna, TX 78537
512-464-3736

DAWSON
Dawson Boats
3909 Mobile Hiway
Pensacola, FL 32505
904-438-5883

DECK-BOAT
Deck Boat Corp.
Box 269
Gatesville, TX 76528

DECK-CRAFT
Harris Deck-Craft
2801 W. State Street
Ft. Wayne, IN 46808

DEL MAGIC
Delco Fbg. Products Inc.
P.O. Box 10
Joshua, TX 76058
817-295-3741

MANUFACTURER'S ADDRESSES (BOAT)

DELTA
Delta Boat Works
Port Canaveral
P.O. Box 947
Cape Canaveral, FL 32920
305-783-3536

DIXIE
Dixie Boat Works
Box 729
Newton, NC 28658
704-464-1961

DIXIE DEVIL
Hermann Boat Works Inc.
P.O. Box 182
Hermann, MO 65041

DIXIE DORY
Alcom Marine, Inc.
P.O. Box 963
Maitland, FL 37251

DOLPHIN (20' Boats)
Dolphin 20' Boats, Inc.
P.O. Box 1401
Homestead, FL 33030
305-248-9668

DOLPHIN (ILLINOIS)
Dolphin Boats Ltd.
2306 Commonwealth
North Chicago, IL 60064
312-473-3434

DOLPHIN (MINN.)
Dolphin Products, Inc.
P.O. Box 230
Wabasha, MN 55981
612-565-3868

DONZI
Donzi Marine, Inc.
2740 N.W. 29th Terrace
Lauderdale Lakes, FL 33311
305-486-3111

DRIFTER
House Boating Corp. of America
365 Maple Street
Gallatin, TN 37066

DURACRAFT
Duracraft Boats, Inc.
Rt. 2
Monticello, AR 71655
501-367-5311

DURANAUTIC
Duranautic Boats Inc.
Van Wyck Lane
Wappinger Falls, NY 12590
914-226-2090

DUROBOAT
Duroboat Manufacturing Co. Inc.
1140 S.W. Dakota St.
Seattle, WA 98106
206-937-3876

DUSKY
Dusky Boats
110 N. Bryan Rd.
Dania, FL 38004

DYNAMAGLAS
Dynamaglas Boat Co.
1661½ County Line Road
Sarasota, FL 33580

EBBTIDE
Ebbtide Corp.
Jones Creek Rd.
White Bluff, TN 37187

EBKO
Ebko Ind. Inc.
P.O. Box 1123
Hastings, NE 68901
402-463-3141

EGG HARBOR
Egg Harbor Boat Co.
801 Philadelphia Ave.
Egg Harbor City, NJ 08215
609-965-2300

ELDOCRAFT
El Do-Craft Boat Co., Inc.
P.O. Box 41
Smackover, AR 71762
501-725-2204

EXCALIBUR
Excalibur Marine
2001 County Rd.
Sarasota, FL 33580
813-355-2711

FAIRLINE
Fairline Boats Ltd.
4087 Victoria Ave.
Niagara Falls, Ontario
Canada L2E 4B2

F.E.C.
F.E.C. Aluminum Products
2765 Niagara Lane
Minneapolis, MN 55441
612-559-5200

FIBERFORM
Fiberform Div.
U.S. Industries, Inc.
Bldg. 20, Spokane Ind. Park
P.O. Box 14647
Spokane, WA 99214

FIBERFORM
See BAYLINER

FIESTA
Fiesta Boats
10298 W. Broadway
Mesa, AZ 85202
602-890-1920

FISHER MARINE
Fisher Marine, Inc.
P.O. Box 1256
West Point, MS 39773
601-494-1786

FISHMASTER
RSB Fiberglass Forms, Inc.
Box 842
La Grange, GA 30240

FLEETCRAFT
Flotilla Corp.
P.O. Box 194B
Woodbine, NJ 08270

FLOTE—BOTE
Harris Mfg. Corp.
2801 State Blvd.
Fort Wayne, IN 46808

FORESTER
Forester Boats, Inc.
Industrial Park, Box 366
Wyoming, MN 55092
612-226-1121

4 WINNS
Saf-T-Mate, Inc.
925 Frisbie Street
Cadillac, MI 49601
616-775-1351

FUN MASTER
Pollard's Enterprises, Inc.
Box 966
Palmetto, FL 33561

FUN-TOON
Muncie Metal Spinning Co.
1012 East 20th St.
Muncie, IN 47302

GALAXIE
Galaxie Boatworks Inc.
P.O. Box 608
Jacksonville, TX 75766
214-586-2563

GALAXY
Galaxy Boat Mfg. Co., Inc.
P.O. Box 3848
Columbia, SC 29230
803-786-2760

GATOR
Moore Ent. Inc.
Highway 80 East
Haughton, LA 71010

GEORGIAN
Georgian Steel Boats, Ltd.
5770 Murie Street
Niagara Falls, Ont., Can. L2E 6X8

GLASSMASTER
Glassmaster Boat Co.
Box 788
Lexington, SC 29072
803-359-2594

MANUFACTURER'S ADDRESSES (BOAT)

GLASSPAR
Larson Industries, Inc.
702 W. River Road
Little Falls, MN 56345

GLASSPORT
Waitsboro Mfg. Co. Inc.
P.O. Box 669
Corbin, KY 40701
606-523-1313

GLASSTREAM
Glasstream Boats, Inc.
P.O. Box 943
Nashville, GA 31639-0943
912-686-2128

GLASTRON
Glastron Boat Co.
Box 9447
Austin, TX 78766-9447
512-341-7792

GLASTRON/CARLSON
See GLASTRON

GRADY-WHITE
Grady White Boats, Inc.
Box 1527
Greenville, NC 27834
919-752-2111

GREAT CANADIAN
Great Canadian Canoes
45 Water Street
Worcester, MA 01604
617-755-5237

GREGOR
Gregor Boat Co.
3564 No. Hazel Ave.
Fresno, CA 93711
209-226-2331

GREW
Grew Boats
Box 760
Penetanguishene, Ont., Canada
L0K 1P0

GRUMMAN
Grumman Boats
Marathon, NY 13803
607-849-3211

HAMMOND
Hammond Boats
P.O. Box 6427
Austin, TX 78762
512-385-8535

HAPPY TRAVELER
Happy Traveler Marine
R.R. 5, Box 201A
Tifton, GA 31794
912-533-4935

HARBOR CRAFT
Div. Holiday Rambler Corp.
P.O. Box 564
Wakarusa, IN 46573
219-862-2653

HARBOR MASTER
House Boating Corp. of America
365 Maple Street
Gallatin, TN 37066
615-452-4343

HARLEY
Harley Boat Corp.
895 E. Gay St.
Bartow, FL 33830
813-533-2800

HATTERAS
AMF Hatteras Yachts
2100 Kivett Drive
High Point, NC 27261
919-885-6051

HAWAIIAN (CA)
Hawaiian Boats Inc.
15571 Container Lane
Huntington Beach, CA 92649

HAWAIIAN (OH)
Hawaiian Boats Inc.
14615 St. Rt. 13 S.W.
Thornport, OH 43076

HAWKLINE
Hawkline Boats
10 Perseverance Lane
Westport, MA 02790

HEADCRAFT
Headcraft, Inc.
4214 Felter at Burleson Rd.
Austin, TX 78744

HEWESCRAFT
Hewes Marine Co.
Rte. 4, Box 315
Colville, WA 99114
509-684-2523

HOBIE
Hobie Cat Div. of Coleman
P.O. Box 1008
Oceanside, CA 92056
714-758-9100

HOLIDAY
Eagle River Boat Works Inc.
18022 Edison Avenue
Chesterfield, MO 63017

HOLIDAY MANSION
Holiday Mansion Div.
Mohawk Inc.
2328 Hein Road
Salina, KS 67401

HURRICANE
Godfrey Conveyor Co.
22787 C.R. 14
Elkhart, IN 46514

HURST
Hurst Enterprises, Inc.
901 Central Florida Pkwy.
Orlando, FL 32809

HUSTLER (IL)
U.S. Fiberglass Corp.
4016 Crystal Lake Rd.
McHenry, IL 60050
815-385-4058

HUSTLER (LA)
Hustler Boat Co.
P.O. Box 5975
Bossier City, LA 71010

HYDRA-SPORTS
Hydra-Sports, Inc.
100 Oceanside Dr.
Nashville, TN 37204
615-385-3652

HYDRODYNE
Crosby Marine Engrg. Corp.
Box 65
Spencerville, IN 46788

HYDROSTREAM
W. E. Pipkorn Mfg. Co.
2211 W. Co. Road D
New Brighton, MN 55112
612-633-3402

I.M.P.
IMP Boats
P.O. Box 347
Iola, KS 66749
714-831-7399

IMPERIAL
All Season Ind., Inc.
Box 327
Markle, IN 46770
219-758-2161

INDIAN
Rivers & Gilman Moulded
Prod. Inc.
P.O. Box 206
Hampden, ME 04444

INVADER
Invader Corp.
Box 420
Giddings, TX 78942
409-542-3101

JAY BEE
Jay Bee Boats
Box 803
Danville, KY 40422
606-236-5601

MANUFACTURER'S ADDRESSES (BOAT)

J. C. PONTOON
J. C. Manufacturing Inc.
State Road 13 North, Route 1
North Webster, IN 46555

JERSEY
New Jersey Boat Works, Inc.
P.O. Box 395
Medford, NJ 08055
609-267-2081

JOHN ALLMAND
John Allmand Boats, Inc.
P.O. Box 4910
Hialeah, FL 33014

KAYOT
Kayot, Inc.
Box 789
Mankato, MN 56001

KENNEDY
Kennedy Houseboats, Inc.
Box 338
Miller, SD 57362

KENNEDY KRAFT
Kennedy Kraft, Inc.
304 Siebert Avenue
Destin, FL 32541
904-837-6680

KINGS CRAFT
Kings Craft, Inc.
P.O. Box 2306
Florence, AL 35630

KINGFISHER
Master Molders, Inc.
Box 1210
Clarksville, TX 75426
214-427-3883

KLAMATH
Trailorboat Co., Inc.
P.O. Box 1267
Sonoma, CA 95476
707-938-3777

LAKESCRAFT
Lakes Mfg., Inc.
Box 382
Ypsilanti, MI 48197

LANDAU
Landau Boat Co.
P.O. Box 750
Lebanon, MO 65536
417-532-9126

LAND 'N SEA
Land 'N Sea Craft
720 Laurelwood Road
Santa Clara, CA 95050

LANGFORD
Langford Canoe and
Woodworking, Inc.
5468 Dundas St. W., Suite 202
Islington, Ontario, Canada

LARSON
Larson Industries, Inc.
702 W. River Rd.
Little Falls, MN 56345
612-632-5481

LASER
Laser Boats
Rt. 4, Box 147
Roanoke, TX 76262
817-491-2802

LAZY DAYS
Lazy Days Mfg. Co., Inc.
6000 Holiday Road
Buford, GA 30518

LEGEND
See Baretta

LEISURE CRAFT
Cron Houseboats
802 Hearn Street
Gallatin, TN 37066

LINCOLN
Lincoln Canoes
Rt. 32
Waldoboro, ME 04572
207-832-5323

LOWE LINE
Lowe Industries
Interstate 44
Lebanon, MO 65536
417-532-9101

LUCRAFT
Lucraft Boats
Box 6335
Daytona Beach, FL 32022

LUHRS
Luhrs Co.-Div. Starcraft Inc.
2703 College Ave.
Goshen, IN 46526

LUND
Lund American, Inc.
Box 248
New York Mills, MN 56567
218-385-2235

LYMAN
Lyman Inc.
1615 First St.
P.O. Box 1209
Sandusky, OH 44870
419-625-4755

MACH I
Felt Enterprises
600 West 10th Ave.
Monmouth, IL 61462
309-734-2175

MACKIE
Mackie Boats
Box 672, Hwy. 98 East
Wake Forest, NC 27587

MAD RIVER
Mad River Canoe
P.O. Box 610
Waitsfield, VT 05673

MAGNUM
Magnum Marine
2900 N.E. 188th St.
No. Miami Beach, FL 33180
305-931-4292

MAKO
Mako Marine, Inc.
4355 N.W. 128th St.
Miami, FL 33054
305-685-6591

MALIBU (Calif.)
Malibu Boats
411 West Ave.
Merced, CA 95340

MALIBU (FLorida)
990 E. Plant St.
Winter Garden, FL 32787
305-656-3622

MANATEE
Manatee Marine Products, Inc.
P.O. Box 6
Palmetto, FL 33561
813-746-8330

MANSON
Manson Boat Works, Inc.
68 Bridge Rd.
Salisbury, MA 01950
617-462-2362

MARATHON
Marathon Boat Co.
Box 186
Kershaw, SC 29067
803-475-6557

MARINETTE
Aluminum Cruisers, Inc.
Standiford Field
Louisville, KY 40213
502-366-1401

MARK TWAIN
Mark Twain Ind., Inc.
Box 276
West Frankfort, IL 62896
618-932-3148

MARLIN
Marlin Boats, Inc.
8251 14th Avenue
White City, OR 97501
503-826-3539

MARQUIS
See Citation

MANUFACTURER'S ADDRESSES (BOAT)

MASTER CRAFT
Mastercraft Boat Co., Inc.
Rt. #9
Maryville, TN 37801
615-983-2178

McKEE CRAFT
Lanness K. McKee & Co.
Box 623
Fairmont, NC 28340
919-628-7940

MEYERS
Myers Industries, Inc.
Tecumseh-Clinton Rd.
P.O. Box 188
Tecumseh, MI 49286
517-423-2151

MFG
Molded Fiberglass Co.
P.O. Box 675
Ashtabula, OH 44004
216-997-5851

MICHI-CRAFT
Michi-Craft Corp.
20000 19 Mile Rd.
Big Rapids, MI 49307
616-796-2675

MIRRO CRAFT
Northport Inc.
39 N. Harding Ave.
Gillett, WI 54124
414-855-2168

MITCHELL
Mitchell Boat Co.
P.O. Box 88
Tallevast, FL 33588

MITCH-CRAFT
Mitchell Boat Co.
2357 Whitfield Ave. E
Sarasota, FL 33580
813-355-2777

MONARK
Monark Boat Co.
Box 210
Monticello, AR 71655
501-367-5361

MONZA
Monza Marine
785 West 25th St.
Hialeah, FL 33010
305-887-5791

MUSTANG
Mustang Boat Co., Inc.
Box 79490
Ft. Worth, TX 76179

NAUTA-LINE
Nauta-Craft, Inc.
Albert Brewer Drive
Lexington, AL 35648

NEWMAN
Newman Fine Boats Inc.
P.O. Box 1208
Miami, OK 74354
918-542-4474

NITRO
P.O. Box 946
Gladewater, TX 75647
214-845-6231

NO. AMERICAN
North American Boat Corp.
3355 S.W. 2nd Ave.
Fort Lauderdale, FL 33315

NORDIC
Nordic Boats
800 N. Lake Havasu Avenue
Lake Havasu City, AZ 86403

OLD TOWN
Old Town Canoe Co.
385 Beaver St.
Old Town, ME 04468
207-827-5513

OMEGA (CA)
Omega Boats, Inc.
4640 E. La Palma Ave.
Anaheim, CA 92807

OMEGA (FL)
Florida Boats, Inc.
3205 N.E. 188th St.
No. Miami, FL 33163

OMNI
Fiberglass Ind. Inc.
P.O. Drawer M
Lecompte, LA 71346

ORRION
Orrion Boats
8269 Alpine Ave.
Sacramento, CA 95826

OSAGIAN
Osagian Boats, Inc.
Hwy. 5 North, Rte. 3, Box 213
Lebanon, MO 65536

OZARK
Ozark Boat Works, Inc.
Industrial Park
Mountain View, MO 65548
417-934-2031

PACEMAKER
See EGG HARBOR

PACIFICA
Pacifica by Kipper Yachts
3595 Frankford
Panama City, FL 32405
904-769-8976

PANTERA
Pantera Marine Inc.
4405 N.W. 73rd Avenue
Miami, FL 33166

PENN YAN
Penn Yan Boats, Inc.
Wadell Ave.
Penn Yan, NY 14527
315-536-4401

PEQUOD
Marine Technology Corp.
Concord Industrial Park
Concord, NH 03301
603-224-5992

PERFORMANCE
Performance Plus Products, Ltd.
P.O. Box 5638
Greenville, MS 38701
601-335-9227

PERMA-CRAFT
Perma-Craft Boat Corp.
1321 South 30th Ave.
Hollywood, FL 30020

PETERSON
Peterson Mfg. Co.
Rte. 1, Box 164
Jackson Gap, AL 36861
205-825-7561

PHANTOM
Phantom Boats Inc.
916 N. Palestine Street
Athens, TX 75751
214-675-5602

PHOENIX
Phoenix Marine Ent., Inc.
1775 W. Okeechobee Road
Hialeah, FL 33010
305-887-5625

PISCES
Pisces Boat Co.
P.O. Box 15593
Tampa, FL 33684

PLAYBUOY
Associated Recreational
1305 S. Cedar
Lansing, MI 88910

PLAY-CRAFT
Play-Craft Pontoon Co.
Box 708
Richland, MO 65556

POLAR KRAFT
Polar Kraft Mfg. Co.
P.O. Box 708
Olive Branch, MS 38654
601-895-5576

MANUFACTURER'S ADDRESSES (BOAT)

PONY
M.N.K. Enterprises, Inc.
P.O. Box 87
Bancroft, ID 83217

POST
Post Marine Co., Inc.
River Road
Mays Landing, NJ 08330
609-625-2434

PRO CRAFT
Malden Craft Inc.
P.O. Box 181
Murfreesboro, TN 37130

PRO-LINE
Pro-Line Inc.
P.O. Box 1348
Crystal River, FL 32629
904-795-4111

QUAPAW
Quapaw Canoe
600 Newman Rd.
Miami, OK 74354
918-542-5536

RALLY
Marlin Boats, Inc.
8251 14th Ave.
White City, OR 97501
503-826-3539

RAMPAGE
Div. of Tillotson-Pearson
2179 St. Road 84
Ft. Lauderdale, FL 33312
305-587-9446

RANGER (CA)
General Marine Co. Div. of
Western States Marine Products
1346 S. Claudina
Anaheim, CA 92805

RANGER/RAWHIDE
Wood Mfg. Co. Inc.
P.O. Box 262
Flippin, AR 72634
501-453-2222

RAWHIDE
Florence Reinforced
Plastics Inc.
Route 3, Box 64
Rogersville, AL 35652

RAY-CRAFT
San Augustine Fbg., Inc.
P.O. Drawer 596
San Augustine, TX 75972
713-275-3456

REGAL
Regal Marine Industries, Inc.
2300 Jetport Drive
Orlando, FL 32809
305-896-0501

REGATTA
Regatta Boats
11402 Brookshire Ave.
Downey, CA 90241
213-869-1536

REGENCY
All Season Ind., Inc.
Box 327
Markle, IN 46770
219-758-2161

RENEGADE
Hosea Mfg. Co.
P.O. Box 609
Quitman, TX 75783

RENKEN
Renken Boat Mfg. Co., Inc.
1750 Signal Point Road
Charleston, SC 29412
803-795-1150

RHYAN-CRAFT
Rhyan-Craft Boat Mfg. Co.
P.O. Box 1537
El Dorado, AR 71730
501-863-4160

RICKBORN
Rickborn Ind. Inc.
175 Atlantic City Blvd.
Bayville, NJ 08721
201-349-4545

RINKERBUILT
Rinker Boat Co. Inc.
Box 208
Syracuse, IN 46567
219-457-3433

RIVIERA CRUISER
Riviera Cruiser Div.
LML Engr. & Mfg. Corp.
607-617 So. Chauncey St.
Columbia City, IN 46725

RIVER OX
See SEA OX

ROBALO
Cobia Boat Co.
P.O. Box 1857
Sanford, FL 32771

ROUGHNECK
Roughneck Boat Co.
P.O. Box 511
Smackover, AR 71762

SANGER
Sanger Boat Mfg.
P.O. Box 10168
Fresno, CA 93725
209-485-2842

SANPAN
Godfrey Conveyor Co., Inc.
22787 Country Road 14
Elkhart, IN 46514

SAWYER
Sawyer Canoe Co.
234 South State
Oscoda, MI 48750
517-739-9181

SEA ARROW
Sea Arrow Marine Corp.
709 Rust
San Angelo, TX 76903

SEA BIRD
Sea Bird Yacht Corp.
1901 S.W. 31st Ave.
Pembroke Park, FL 33009
305-966-9475

SEACAMPER
Seacamper Industries Inc.
P.O. Box 1379
Palatka, FL 32077

SEACRAFT
Sea Craft, Inc.
P.O. Box 4040
24400 S.W. 137 Ave.
Princeton, FL 33032

SEA KING
Montgomery Ward
619 West Chicago Ave.
Chicago, IL 60671

SEA NYMPH
Sea Nymph Mfg. Corp.
P.O. Box 337
Syracuse, IN 46567
219-457-3131

SEA OX
North American
Fiberglass Corp.
Industrial Park
P.O. Drawer C
Greenville, NC 27834
919-758-9901

SEA RAIDER
Sea Raider Boats Inc.
P.O. Box 712
Sandusky, OH 44870
419-626-5510

SEA RAY
Sea Ray Boats
4140 E. Raymond
Phoenix, AZ 85040
602-268-1301

SEARS
Sears, Roebuck & Co.
Sears Tower
Chicago, IL 60684

SEA-SAFE
Sea-Safe Marine Inc.
Route 8, Williams Road
Monroe, NC 28110

MANUFACTURER'S ADDRESS (BOAT)

SEA SPRITE
Sea Sprite Boat Co., Inc.
P.O. Box 430
Crescent City, IL 60928-0430
815-683-2155

SEA SQUIRT
VIP Marine Ind.
3798 Ravenswood Rd.
Ft. Lauderdale, FL 33312
305-581-5451

SEA STAR
Glastex Co.
600 West 10th Ave.
Monmouth, IL 61462
309-734-2175

SEA SWIRL
Bramco Inc.
7th & "C" Street, Box 167
Culver, OR 97734
503-546-5011

SEAVILLA
Alloy Mfg., Ltd.
Box 240
Lachine, Que., Canada

SEAWAY
Seaway Boats
P.O. Box 338
Winthrop, ME 04364

SEBRING
Sebring Boats
Div. of C&S Ent.
P.O. Box 236
Cullman, AL 35055

SHAMROCK
Shamrock Marine, Inc.
P.O. Box 1095
Cape Coral, FL 33904
813-574-2800

SIDEWINDER
See THOMPSON

SILVERLINE
See Lund

SILVERTON
Silverton Marine Corp.
120 Kettle Creek Rd.
Toms River, NJ 08753
201-255-1100

SKEETER
Skeeter Products
P.O. Box 230
Kilgore, TX 75662
214-984-0541

SKI BARGE
Dilks & Co.
P.O. Box 70
Knoxville, AR 72845
501-885-2221

SKIFF CRAFT
Henry Boats, Inc.
P.O. Box 115
Plain City, OH 43064
614-873-4664

SKIPJACK (CA)
Skipjack Boats Inc.
1763 Placentia Ave.
Costa Mesa, CA 92627
714-646-2451

SKIPJACK (TN)
Skipjack Boats
703-D S. Cumberland
Lebanon, TN 37087
615-449-5317

SKIPPER CRAFT
Funway Marine Inc.
P.O. Box 88 - Hwy. 28
Plum Branch, SC 29845

SKIPPERLINER
Skipperliner Houseboats
3222 Commerce Street
LaCrosse, WI 54601

SLEEK-CRAFT
Sleek Craft Boats
9620 Santa Fe Springs Road
Santa Fe Springs, CA 90670
213-698-0928

SLICK CRAFT (MI)
See Tiara

SLICK CRAFT (MN)
Slick Craft Boat
Div. of AMF Inc.
609 N.E. 13th Ave.
Little Falls, MN 56345

SMOKER-CRAFT
Smoker Craft, Inc.
Box 65
New Paris, IN 46553
219-831-2103

SOMERSET
Somerset Cruisers
5000 South US 27
Somerset, KY 42501

SONIC
J. R. Custom Marine Inc.
2010 N.W. 29th Street
Ft. Lauderdale, FL 33311

SOUTHWIND
Jen-Craft, Inc.
770 N. Lemon Avenue
Orange, CA 92667

SPECTRA
Spectra Marine
2821 N. Lima Street
Burbank, CA 91504

SPEEDLINER
Seajay Boats, Inc.
4017 River Road
St. Joseph, MO 64505

SPORTCRAFT
Sportcraft, Inc.
P.O. Box 351
Perry, FL 32347
904-584-5679

SPORTMASTER
RSB Fiberglass Forms, Inc.
P.O. Box 842
La Grange, GA 30240
404-882-1438

SPORTSPAL
Sportspal, Inc.
Industrial Park Rd.
Johnstown, PA 16373

STALLION
Stallion Marine Inc.
5980 Lakehurst Dr.
Orlando, FL 32819
305-352-6067

STAMAS
Stamas Boats, Inc.
300 Pampas Ave.
Tarpon Springs, FL 33589
813-937-4118

STAR
Star Boat Co.
P.O. Box 758
Gulf Breeze, FL 32561

STARCRAFT
Starcraft Marine
W. Starcraft Drive
Topeka, IN 46571
219-593-2550

STARFIRE
Starfire Boats
619 So. 600 W.
Salt Lake City, UT 84101
801-355-2949

STERLING
Sterling Marine, Inc.
P.O. Box 13014-A
Orlando, FL 32859
305-656-7474

STERNCRAFT
Sterncraft Boat Co.
Hwy. 121 East
Lewisville, TX 75067

STEURY
Viking Boat Co.
P.O. Box 85
310 Steury Ave.
Goshen, IN 46526

MANUFACTURER'S ADDRESSES (BOAT)

STINGER
Stinger Boats, Inc.
1011 W. Kirkland
Nashville, TN 37216

STINGRAY
Stingray Boat Co.
P.O. Box 669
Hartsville, SC 29550
803-383-4507

STOTT CRAFT
Stott Craft Boat Co.
P.O. Box 158
Soddy-Daisy, TN 37379

STRYKER
R&R Fbg. Co.
Hwy. 72 West, Route 2
Madison, AL 35758

SUCCESS
Mel-Hart Products Inc.
1052 Harrison Street
Conway, AR 72032
800-643-8369

SUNRAY (Calif.)
Arrivee Performance Yachts, Inc.
1346 S. Claudina St.
Anaheim, CA 92805
714-991-4021

SUNRAY (CANADA)
Sunray Boats, Inc.
355 Labbe Blvd.
P.O. Box 544
Victoriaville, Quebec, Canada
G6P 1B1

SUN RUNNER
Sun Runner Marine
South 6012 Hayford Rd.
Spokane, WA 99204
509-244-3611

SUN TRACKER
Bass Pro Shops
P.O. Box 4046
Springfield, MO 65808-4046
1-800-227-7776

SUPRA
Supra Sports Inc.
P.O. Box C
Greenback, TN 37742
615-856-3035

SUPREME
Supreme Ind. Inc.
Route 4, New Top Side Road
Louisville, TN 37777
615-984-7700

SUTPHEN
Sutphen Marine Corp.
923 S.E. 13th Ave.
Cape Coral, FL 33904
813-542-0554

SWITZER
SCI Corp.
7109 Pingree Rd.
Crystal Lake, IL 60014
815-459-2460

SYLVAN
Sylvan Marine
P.O. Box 25
New Paris, IN 46553
219-831-2950

TAHITI
Bell Industries
17906 Crusader Avenue
Orange, CA 90701

TAYLOR
Fiberglass Prod., Inc.
14102 Ramona Blvd.
Baldwin Park, CA 91706

TAYLORCRAFT
Taylor Craft Ind. Inc.
Route 2, Box 20
Burkesville, KY 42717

TERRY
See STARCRAFT

THOMPSON
Thompson Boat, Inc.
900 Chesaning
St. Charles, MI 48655
517-865-9968

THUNDERBIRD/FORMULA
Thunderbird Products Corp
P.O. Box 501
Decatur, IN 46733
219-724-9111

THUNDER BOLT
Thunder Bolt Boats Inc.
Rte. 1, Box 569
Cleburne, TX 76031

THUNDERCRAFT
Thundercraft Boats Inc.
P.O. Box 5185
Knoxville, TN 37918
615-687-3410

TIARA
Tiara Power Div.
of S2 Yachts, Inc.
725 E. 40th St.
Holland, MI 49423
616-392-7163

TIDE CRAFT
Tide Craft, Inc.
P.O. Box 878
Minden, LA 71055
318-377-5703

TOLLYCRAFT
Tollycraft Corp.
2200 Clinton Ave.
Kelso, WA 98626
206/423-5160

TOM-KAT
Kincaid Distributing, Inc.
P.O. Box 173
Hwy. 60 East
Barlow, FL 33830

TOPAZ
Topaz Marine Corp.
3 Binnacle Lane
Owings, MD 20836
301-257-3101

TRI-SONIC
Div. V.I.P.
4025 Marina Dr.
Ft. Worth, TX 76135

TROJAN
Trojan Boat Co.
P.O. Box 3571
Lancaster, PA 17603
717-397-2471

TUFFY
Glasway, Inc.
865 E. Stony Rd.
Lake Mills, WI 53551
414-648-2348

TUNNEL CRAFT
OME Inc.
1216 S.W. 6th Avenue
Ocala, FL 32670

TWIN-ALUME
Brown-Hutchinson, Inc.
1831 Clay Avenue
Detroit, MI 48211

UNIFLITE
Uniflite, Inc.
P.O. Box 1095
Bellingham, WA 98225
206-676-6200

VALCO
Hulls, Inc.
7028 Minnewawa Ave.
Clovis, CA 93612
209-299-9551

VAPOR VETTE
Delta West Mfg.
P.O. Box 228
Lodi, CA 95241
209-334-3166

VENTURE
Venture Boats, Inc.
Rt. 2 - Elk River Rd.
Winchester, TN 37398
615-967-5567

MANUFACTURER'S ADDRESSES (BOAT)

VIKING
Viking Boat Co., Inc.
310 Steury Ave.
P.O. Box 85
Goshen, IN 46526

V.I.P.
Vivian Industrial Plastics, Inc.
P.O. Box 232
Vivian, LA 71082
318-375-3241

WARREN PRODUCTS
Warren Prod., Inc.
275 Market St.
Warren, IN 46792

WEBBCRAFT
Webbcraft Inc.
P.O. Box 10
Collinsville, OK 74021
918-371-3655

WEERES
Weeres Industries, Inc.
Box 98
St. Cloud, MN 56301

WELLCRAFT
Wellcraft Marine Corp.
8151 Bradenton Rd.
Sarasota, FL 33580
813-753-7811

WENZEL
Wenzel Fiberglass Boat Co., Inc.
Rt. 1, Deep Creek Lake
McHenry, MD 21541

WESTCOASTER
See Klamath

WILDERNESS PRODUCTS
Wilderness Products Co., Inc.
P.O. Box 93
Cumming, GA 30130

WILLARD
The Willard Co.
11200 Condor Ave.
Fountain Valley, CA 92708
714-540-5211

WINDSONG
Windsong Boat Co.
Div. of Trend Mfg. Co.
P.O. Box 6805
Jacksonville, FL 32205

WINNER (MI)
See THOMPSON

WINNER (NC)
Winner Boats
P.O. Box 1027
Mt. Pleasant, NC 28124
704-436-9363

WITCHCRAFT
Metropolitan Marine Inc.
P.O. Box 297
Rialto, CA 92376

WRIEDT
Southwest Fbg.
6609 Coffeyville Hwy.
Coffeyville, TX 76034

YAR-CRAFT
Yar-Craft, Inc.
1104 20th Ave.
Menominee, MI 49858
906-863-6350

YAZOO
Aladdin Mfg. Co.
466 Bridge Street West
P.O. Box 308
Yazoo City, MS 39194
601-746-7481

MANUFACTURER'S ADDRESSES

OUTBOARD MOTOR

AQUABUG
Aquabug Int'l., Inc.
100 Merrick Rd.
Rockville Centre, NY 11570
516-536-8217

ARROW TRITON
TMC Products-Triton Marine
754 Wellington St.
Montreal, Quebec, Canada
H3C 1T4
514-866-3331

BRITISH SEAGULL
Inland Marine Co.
79 E. Jackson St.
P.O. Box 1323
Wilkes-Barre, PA 18703
717-822-7185

CARNITI
Pennsylvania Development Co.
3810 Crooked Run Road
North Versailles, PA 15137
412-471-4181

CHRYSLER
Bayliner Marine Corp.
P.O. Box 24467
Seattle, WA 98134

CLINTON & CHIEF
Clinton Engines Corp.
Clark & Maple Streets
Maquoketa, IA 52060

CRUISE 'N CARRY
HMC, Inc.
20710 Alameda St.
Long Beach, CA 90810
213-603-9888

ESKA
The Eska Company
2400 Kerper Boulevard
Dubuque, IA 52001
319-556-4460

EVINRUDE
Evinrude Motors
P.C. Box 663
Milwaukee, WI 53201
414-445-0643

EXPLORER
See Eska

FORCE
U.S. Marine Corp.
P.O. Box 24467
Seattle, WA 98134

HONDA
Honda Motor Co., Inc.
100 West Alondra Blvd.
Gardena, CA 90247
213-321-8680

JOHNSON
Johnson Outboards
200 Sea-horse Drive
Waukegan, IL 60085
312-689-6200

MAG
See Minn-Kota

MARINER
Mariner Outboards
1939 Pioneer Road
Fond du Lac, WI 54935
414-923-3200

MERCURY
Mercury Marine
1939 Pioneer Rd.
Fond du Lac, WI 54935
414-929-5000

MIGHTY MITE
Mighty Mite Inc.
Colton Rd.
Old Lyme, CT 06371
813-369-4752

MINN KOTA
1531 Madison Ave.
Mankato, MN 56001
218-233-7276

MOTOR GUIDE
P.O. Box 825
Starkville, MS 39759
601-323-1521

RAM
Ram Products, Inc.
P.O. Box 1537
618 East Markham
Little Rock, AR 72203

SEA KING
Montgomery Ward
619 W. Chicago Ave.
Chicago, IL 60607

SEARS
Sears Roebuck & Co.
Sears Tower
Chicago, IL 60684

SILVERTROL
Silvertrol Industries, Inc.
P.O. Box H
Pierce City, MO 65723

SPIRIT
See Suzuki

SUZUKI
Suzuki International, Inc.
3251 E. Imperial Hwy.
P.O. Box 1100
Brea, CA 92621
714-996-7040

TANAKA
Tanaka Kogyo U.S.A.
7509 S. 228th St.
Kent, WA 98031
206-854-7706

TOHATSU
Tohatsu, U.S.A.
1211 Ave. of the Americas
New York, NY 10036
212-704-6722

VOLVO PENTA
AB Volvo Penta of America, Inc.
Bldg. A, Rockleigh Ind. Park
Rockleigh, NJ 07647

WIZARD
Western Auto Supply Co.
2107 Grand Avenue
Kansas City, MO 64108

YAMAHA
6555 Katella Ave.
Cypress, CA 90630
714-761-7396

MANUFACTURER'S ADDRESSES
INBOARD ENGINE AND STERN DRIVE

BMW
BMW of North America, Inc.
Walnut & Hudson Streets
Norwood, NJ 07648

CHRYSLER
Chrysler Marine
6565 E. Eight Mile Rd.
Warren, MI 48091

CRUSADER
Thermo Electron, Div. Crusader
7100 East 15 Mile Rd.
Sterling Heights, MI 48077

FORD
Ford Industrial Engines Operations
300 Renaissance Center
Detroit, MI 48243

MARINE DRIVE SYSTEMS
Marine Drive Systems, Inc.
519 Raritan Center
Edison, NJ 08817

MERCRUISER
Mercury Marine
1939 Pioneer Rd.
Fond du Lac, WI 54935

OMC
OMC Drive Systems
3145 Central Ave.
Waukegan, IL 60085

PLEASURECRAFT
Pleasurecraft Marine Engine Co.
P.O. Box 130
7515 Hill Rd.
Canal Winchester, OH 43110

UNIVERSAL
Medalist Universal Motors
1552 Harrison Street
Oshkosh, WI 54903

VOLVO
Volvo Penta of America, Inc.
P.O. Box 174
Rockleigh, NJ 07647

WESTERBEKE
J.H. Westerbeke Corporation
Avon Industrial Park
Avon, MA 02322

INBOARD DRIVE

HURTH
Trigon Machinery
214 Brunswick Boulevard
Pointe Claire, Quebec, Canada

PARAGON
Paragon Power, Inc.
7455 Tyler Blvd.
Mentor, OH 44060

TWIN DISC
Twin Disc
1328 Racine Street
Racine, WI 53403

VELVET DRIVE
Warner Gear Division
P.O. Box 2688
Muncie, IN 47302

JET DRIVE

BERKELEY
Berkeley Pump Company
829 Bancroft Way
Berkeley, CA 94710

CHRYSLER
Chrysler Marine
6565 E. Eight Mile Rd.
Warren, MI 48091

JACUZZI
North American Marine Jet
P.O. Box 1232
Benton, AR 72015

OMC
OMC Drive Systems
3145 Central Ave.
Waukegan, IL 60085

INDEX